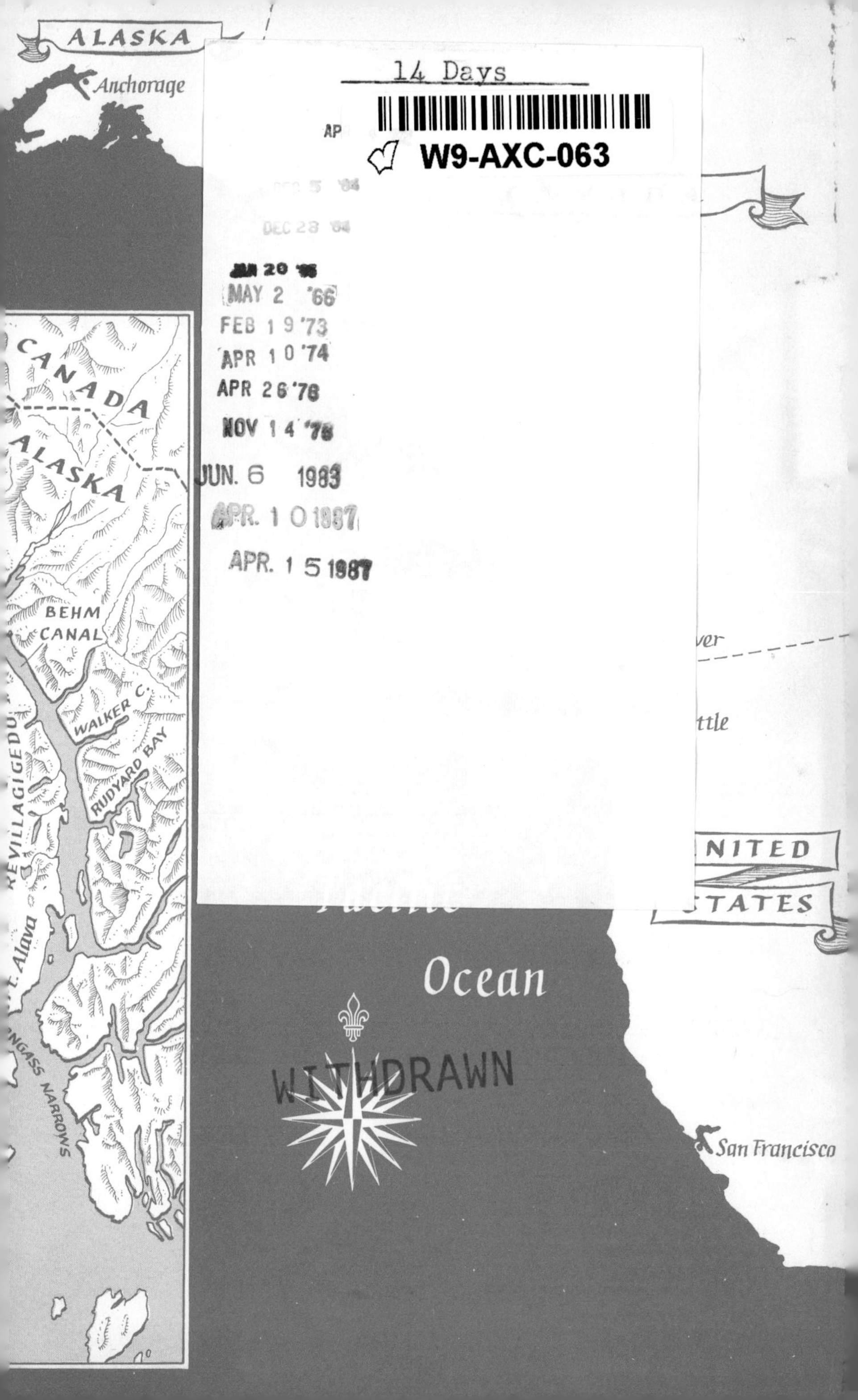
ALASKA
Anchorage
CANADA
ALASKA
BEHM CANAL
WALKER C.
RUDYARD BAY
REVILLAGIGEDO
Pt. Alava
NARROWS
Ocean
San Francisco
NITED
STATES

A CREW OF TWO

BETH EBERHART

Like most women, Beth Eberhart would choose a comfortable, tidy home with congenial neighbors and relatively certain expectations of what the morrow will bring. Like most men, her husband, Vady, prefers to explore the unknown, to seek out new frontiers, to live with challenge and danger rather than with hot meals and soft beds. And so, since the Eberharts are a devoted couple, it is not too surprising that Beth one year found herself windblown and jean-clad, navigating a willful boat through turbulent waters, confined all day in quarters no larger than an outhouse, or playing poker with a group of Haida Indians on a scroungy fish-buying scow. For what happened is that Beth and Vady Eberhart, though greenhorns, undertook to become commercial fishermen operating their own troller off the coast of Alaska.

In A CREW OF TWO, Beth gives us a warm, humorous, inevitably exciting account of their personal experiences as they pursued an adventure men dream of and women dread. Though Beth frankly feared the sea, she was all too soon steering her way through sudden storms, hidden reefs, tricky currents, dense fogs. Since they were trying to make a living out of this venture, reluctant fish and the loss of expensive equipment were among their crucial problems. Engine failure was not only an exasperatingly common occurrence but also a genuine danger inasmuch

(continued on the back flap)

A CREW OF TWO

by Beth Eberhart

ILLUSTRATED BY THE AUTHOR

DOUBLEDAY & COMPANY, INC. GARDEN CITY, NEW YORK
1961

Library of Congress Catalog Card Number 61–8791

Printed in the United States of America
First Edition

TO ETHEL DASSOW,
a dear friend and able editor,
with warmest appreciation for invaluable assistance.

A CREW OF TWO

Chapter 1

Sometimes on stormy evenings when our house trembles from a gusty blast whistling down the gap from Mount Rainier, Vady says, "I'm glad we're not bucking this southeaster around Cape Chacon tonight!"

In his devious way my husband is telling me he loves me.

"Or holed up in Breezy Bay with you standing anchor watch all night," I say. Again I see the *Emblem* pounding on the rocks in McHenry Anchorage, and that last dreadful day on the Coronation Flats.

"What I wouldn't give . . ." he begins, then stops with a rueful smile.

"To be back in Alaska with the fishing fleet," I finish

for him, knowing so well there's no place he'd rather be.

Nevertheless, he is accepting the present both philosophically and happily. He's willing to call it my turn.

Before I met Vady I thought marriage meant settling down. You had children, reared them to the best of your ability, then retired to gentle pursuits and hobbies neglected during the busy years.

I knew exactly what I'd do. Water-color painting was a fascinating hobby. I'd paint.

"Oh no!" Vady would protest. "That's not the end. When the children leave home, it's the beginning. We'll be free of responsibilities, free to take up where we left off, go on to new opportunities and adventures. Of course we'll have hobbies, and time to enjoy them. The possibilities are endless!"

Would I have hesitated if I could have seen myself twenty-five years later? Not as I liked to imagine, a middle-aged housewife in a snug little home, or perhaps even an artist dabbling over a potential masterpiece, but as a greenhorn navigator, wind-blow and jean-clad, playing poker with a group of Haida Indians on a scroungy fish-buying boat?

Of course I wouldn't have hesitated. Young people in love don't worry much about the future.

During the first twenty years of our marriage it was his turn. We moved on an average of once a year while he was successively cowboy, logger, Marine, schoolteacher, bookkeeper, salesman, officer in the Department of Justice, insurance investigator, chief boatswain's mate in the Coast Guard, author, policeman, commercial fisherman, and fish buyer. Each time my home-loving roots protested loudly as we jerked them up for another transplanting. I became an expert packer and unpacker as we followed Vady, the opportunist, in his restless search for the perfect combination of being his own man and making a living for a wife and three children.

We thought one teacher summed it up neatly when Glen turned in an essay on "My Life." "This is not an autobiography," he said, "it's a travelogue."

Then came that frightful day at Pearl Harbor. Our elder daughter, Iris, married a boy in the Army. Glen, seventeen and just out of high school, joined the Navy. Then Vady came home one day and announced he had joined the Coast Guard.

"Oh no!" I wailed. "How could you? You're overage. You fought in one war!"

"Now, now, Beth," he said soothingly, "take it easy. I have to go. A man can't see his only son go into it and stay out himself. Things won't be much different. I'll be based right here in Seattle, and can come home every night."

A few days later, dressed in navy blues with his chief boatswain's cap set at a rakish angle, he posed before me. "How do I look?"

He looked wonderful. So vitally alive, so slim. I was as proud as a sixteen-year-old with her first beau.

Things really weren't much different, at first. Then transfers began coming with haunting regularity. Tacoma, Seattle, back to Tacoma, Inglewood, Quilcene on the Olympic Peninsula, then Alaska!

With Vady gone and Beverly in school all day, I decided to paint again. There hadn't been much time for it, and the few times I'd tried it, Vady, seeming to resent my preoccupation, would suggest a picnic, a ride, or "maybe you and I could do the garden some good." If I said I'd rather paint, he'd slam out of the house with a hurt expression. That wasn't like Vady.

Not that I'm a finished artist, but color and form have

the same effect on me as good music has on many people.

I hunted up the box of paints that had been hidden away for years. The paints were dried and the brushes poor, but I stretched my paper, sketched in a simple seascape for practice, and settled down for a happy afternoon.

Then a strange thing happened. I couldn't paint. It was as if Vady stood there looking over my shoulder.

After an hour's work the graceful boat I had drawn looked as stiff as a dead herring. The turquoise sea, opaque and dull, spawned crests of white marble.

Discouraged and frustrated, I crammed the paints back into the box and got a job at the naval supply depot.

Vady had been in Alaska more than a year, patrolling the outside waters in a converted whaler, when his vessel was sent to the Navy yard in Seattle for repairs. A month's leave! What a month it would be! Glen timed his leave to coincide with his dad's. Iris came home for a visit, bringing our first grandchild.

Two weeks before his leave was up, Vady announced, "I'm taking you and Bev back to Alaska with me."

"How can you when we both have war jobs?" I asked.

"You can quit your jobs."

"But our house! The new furniture, my lovely rug, the first entirely new outfit we've ever had!"

"We'll sell the house furnished."

"Aren't there regulations against servicemen moving their families to the Territory? You said yourself there's a housing shortage in Ketchikan."

"Now, now," Vady said, "calm down, Babe. You won't have to worry about a thing. I rented a couple of rooms before I left."

Two weeks later as we lay in our bunks on the blacked-out ship and heard the "who-o-o" of its bass whistle echoed by the "peep-peep" of a small boat out in the fog, I felt as homeless as a cat in a sack. This time we had severed all ties. We might as well be going to a foreign land.

"This is going to be great," Vady said, sticking his hand out of the upper bunk and groping in the dark for my hand, "having you and Bev with me. You'll love Alaska. It's your kind of country."

Not from what I've heard about it, I thought bleakly.

"It's a country of contrasts," he went on, "raw, new, and untamed."

That didn't sound like my kind of country. I didn't want to tame any wilderness.

"Everywhere are signs of former activity, old mine workings, ruins of canneries, ghost towns with only a few buildings left standing. Roaming through those deep woods, I could imagine I was the last man left on earth."

I didn't want to be the last man on earth, or even the last woman.

"On that patrol last winter we went into bays and harbors you'd never guess were there until we got inside. Some of them weren't even charted."

I didn't want to find out what bays and harbors they'd left off the charts.

"And opportunities! It's chock full of them."

I'd stick it out until after the war was over, then, by golly, we'd go back to Seattle on the very first boat, buy another house, and settle down for good!

"When the war's over," Vady said, "we'll do some scouting around."

Chapter 2

Ketchikan, backed up against the mountain with its feet braced to keep it from slipping into Tongass Narrows, was not at all as I'd imagined it would be. No yelping dog teams, no Eskimos in fur-lined parkas, no blanketed Indian women displaying their hand-woven baskets and beaded moccasins. In fact, it was little different from many small waterfront towns in Washington. A mere six hundred fifty miles had not transported us into the arctic regions.

Pictures of Alaska most widely circulated Outside show towering peaks with glaciers flowing down their sides to end abruptly in iceberg-dotted waters. These pictures were not taken near Ketchikan, where Deer Mountain, its head in the clouds, overlooks the town from a height of three thousand feet.

The mountains here have rounded domes and gracious curves and are so thickly wooded they suggest a pile of pillows under a green plush throw. Spruce and hemlocks nudge one another for standing room only, and old snags, bleached and whitened skeletons, stand out amid the green like exclamation points.

Old-timers claim the climate is like Seattle's. It is, with the similarity a panther has to a nice, soft tabby cat. They don't claim "dry rain," as they do in the Puget Sound area, but, as one old-timer put it, "The rain up here is sort of oily. It just runs off." With a record yearly rainfall of more than sixteen feet, it naturally has to run somewhere.

It was raining when we arrived. Planked streets echoed hollowly beneath the wheels of our taxi as we drove along the waterfront to the rooms Vady had rented. Long gray stairways panted up the steep hillsides to houses almost hidden in the forest. Everything was gray in the fog and rain, the mountains, the water, the sky, even the trees.

House-hunting was even more discouraging than I'd feared. Old buildings, vacant for years, had been remodeled into apartments to accommodate the families of servicemen. Shacks and garages were converted into living quarters. Even these were occupied by healthy-looking people who apparently meant to stay where they were until they died of old age.

Vady, however, wasn't discouraged. "Don't worry, I'll find something," he said, and he did. While Coast Guard acquaintances who had been in Alaska longer than we had been were fretting away the days in hotel rooms, he found a wanigan for sale.

In Alaska a wanigan is usually a floating bunkhouse

for use in out-of-the-way logging camps, but this wanigan was a five-room house on a log float. The foundation of heavy timbers was securely bolted to six huge spruce logs, three on one side, three on the other, with a waterway between for easy towing. A cross-log beneath, in back, compensated for the slope of the beach. From the water it looked like some queer land monster with its mouth wide open, yelling greetings to the boats that passed in Tongass Narrows.

"I'm a hand-logger," said the owner, a little French-Canadian. "I guess you might say I'm a little of everything—hand-logger, fisherman, trapper and hunter. We make our way as we go. The boys and I built this place ourselves. They're right handy with tools. She's built solid and she'll take the weather. We towed her across Clarence Strait last fall with those two trollers of ours, kept her in Chomley while we logged."

It was after midnight when we left, the proud owners of the wanigan. I could hardly drag Vady away.

"You see, Babe," he said as we took our seats on the bus, "that's what I mean. That's what I've been trying to tell you. When a man can live off the land, making his way as he goes, it's darned near a perfect setup."

"As long as it's going to be temporary," I said, "let's make it so gay and cheerful we'll never miss the sunshine."

"Took it over to Chomley," Vady said wonderingly. "Towed it with those two little boats. What say, Babe?"

"I said, let's go all out, make it colorful. Better not be conventional in a place like that. Let's try some new decorating ideas."

"Sure, Betsy. A fellow could set a house like that on the beach anywhere. Use it as headquarters for logging, trapping, even fishing!"

"We'll paper that living room something bright and gaudy."

"There's no end to the possibilities!"

With five rooms and a bath of our own, we were the envy of our acquaintances.

Living in a float house on tidewater brought its problems. During ordinary tides we never floated. Once or twice a month, when the tides reached their maximum heights of fifteen to twenty feet, the wanigan came alive. As the water crept up the beach, creaks and groans announced that we were rising from our resting place on the sand. When there was a wind at the height of the tide, the wanigan would swing on the mooring lines and we might settle several feet to port or starboard of the old bed, with a resultant list in our living quarters.

It is uncomfortable but not impossible to sleep with one's head lower than the feet. We found it more convenient to make up the beds head to foot during such times. I didn't mind the quick little downhill trot to the kitchen sink. It was the uphill climb to the table that made it seem like a long time until the next extreme-high tide, when Vady could get the wanigan back into position.

After he installed a reel clothesline from our back porch to a high piling on the tide flat, washdays were happy days for me. Standing on the porch, smelling the good tang of salt water and new-cut logs from the nearby mill, I could watch the boats passing as I hung up the clothes. Or look across the way to nearby Gravina Island, where the scudding clouds formed interesting patterns on Judy Hill. Most time-killing of all were the ravens, playing in the air currents over the mill. Using the updraft made by the wind against the side of the building, they'd climb to dizzy heights on their airy escalator, then come tumbling down in a series of abandoned falls, twisting and turning like so many big black autumn leaves. They never seemed to tire of this sport, and I never tired of watching them.

One day a man from the mill knocked at the door. "Pardon me, ma'am," he said, "but did you know your clothes are draggin' in the salt chuck?"

No, I hadn't known! Watching the antics of those silly ravens from the kitchen window, I'd forgotten the rising tide. Draggin' they certainly were! Five times those clothes went through the washing machine as I tried to get out the combination of sand that sank to the bottom of the tub and sawdust that floated on the top. I always imagined, afterward, that the seams still felt gritty.

We were so busy reconditioning our new home that we hardly noticed the passing of winter. Spring came on reluctantly, as it always does in Ketchikan, but one day nature asserted herself. She drowned out the lusty smell of the tide flats with the odors of new growth, and warmed the chill rains into balmy spring showers. The wind swung around to the north and the skies cleared. Never had skies seemed so blue! And the water was even bluer, with sparkling waves and dancing whitecaps.

Spring! The season of new beginnings.

We finished the house just in time for Beverly's wedding. Harvey, a Coast Guard boy from Seattle, had become a fixture around the wanigan, and we'd come to love him as our own son. When he and Beverly began making Sunday climbs to the top of Deer Mountain, we knew it was a courtship. Our younger daughter had never been the athletic type.

She told us the big news, then hastened to add, "Of course we wouldn't think of being married before the war is over!"

Three days later she had more news. "We've decided

to be married in about three months. We think June weddings are the nicest."

Her next announcement really crowded the remodeling. "We're going to be married in three weeks. If we put it off until June, he might be transferred overseas and we might never be married."

When the last guest had left after the wedding, Vady and I lingered over a final cup of coffee.

"It'll be lonesome with Bev gone," I said. "The house will seem empty with just the two of us."

There was no reflective nostalgia in Vady's expression. "This is it, Babe. The beginning for us. We've done our duty, if you can call it that, and had a fine time doing it. Now we're free! We'll have time to do all the things we've always wanted to do. Not a worry or a care. From now on, Babe, we live the life of Riley!"

Who was this Riley? Where did he live? How did he live that his life was so enviable? Not knowing who he was, I could only hope what he wasn't. I hoped with all my heart he wasn't a fisherman.

"When I think of all the opportunities! You know, Betsy, with a troller, a fellow wouldn't have to work for someone else."

Chapter 3

During the long spring evenings we sometimes walked up toward the hills, and often surprised a deer browsing in the dense underbrush. Or one might pop out ahead of us, run a few yards along the trail, then melt like a shadow into the foliage.

Sometimes we took a hand line and fished from one of the wharves. A little piece of bacon dangling on a line attracted the bullheads. These luckless fellows, in turn, made good bait for the numerous cod that fed along the piling.

These two pastimes were to humor me. The nights we walked along the waterfront were Vady's choice. He'd bounce along beside me, pointing here, stopping there, chattering away like a self-playing record, pointing out things that never lost their fascination for him. Seeing a troller icing up for a trip at the cold-storage dock, he'd be as excited as a prospector who had just stumbled across the mother lode.

A long chute from the icehouse on the dock was lowered into the hold. Crushed ice tinkled down the metal chute until every inch of space in the hold was filled. As the chute was lifted away, the fisherman would coil his lines on deck and cast off.

"There's a lucky fellow for you," Vady would say, his eyes sparkling. "He'll be out ten days or two weeks, going wherever his fancy takes him, anchored up at night in some little harbor where it's quiet and peaceful. In a place like that you can forget everything."

As we walked on across the bridge spanning Ketchikan Creek, we'd pause while Vady would recount the story of how the Indians had built their village "right here on this very creek." A rock in the center split the water, throwing spray to either side. Seeing a resemblance to a bird, the Indians named their village Kach Khanna, meaning the spread wings of a prostrate eagle. White men, who couldn't contort their mouths to form the guttural Indian sounds, corrupted the name to Ketchikan.

Those houses, marching tipsily along the creek on their high stilt pilings, were once the center of town. But Ketchikan had spread north, and now Creek Street, with its fancy women and drunken men, had fallen into disgrace.

Now we were ready for the climax, the boats! Below us, in the natural bight formed by the mouth of the creek, well protected by a breakwater, lay Thomas Basin, moorage for the hundreds of cruisers and trollers, seiners and skiffs whose home port is Ketchikan.

Down the ramp and onto the floats we'd walk, first to Float A, the aristocrat, proudly displaying the beautiful cruisers. Down one side and up the other we'd go, finally ending up on E with its dilapidated collection of puddle jumpers.

"This is a teakwood boat," Vady would point out. "She's a hundred and eight years old. Used to be a sailing vessel before the present owner converted her to a troller."

"Um-uh."

"Look at this one. Metal. See those rust spots. You never know with a metal boat when she'll spring a leak. They have to be well kept up and painted or they'll rust through. She won't last much longer."

"Um-uh."

"Notice the names. They give a hint of the owner's character. *Taku Wind, Yakobi, Kuiu* and *Adak*. Their owners are probably the adventurous type, dreaming of far-off places. Home lovers name their boats after wives and sweethearts."

"Is the owner of the *Comet* a frustrated aviator? And the *Pumpkin Seed*. Gardener or cook?"

"They were just being fanciful."

"Here's one I like," I continued, pointing to a battered old square-nosed humdirgen. "*Tub*. The fellow who named that was a realist."

Vady walked on and stopped to talk to a man on a small troller. No wonder he knew so much about boats. A walk on the floats was like a cub reporter's beat. He paused for a greeting here, a sociable fifteen minutes there, questions asked and answered with everyone we met.

"Looks like you're about rigged up," he said to a young man busy in his cockpit.

"Yep. We're leaving tomorrow. How's she look to you,

Chief? I couldn't afford gurdies, but this ought to work."

His wire lines, still on the original cardboard spools, had been fitted with gears on the hubs. A bicycle chain attached to a wheel in the cockpit was slipped over the gear. The young man reached out and turned a rough wooden handle. The spool turned slowly and the line tightened in the block.

"Looks fine," Vady said. "Where's your chain for the other side?"

"Not another one in town," the boy answered. "When I catch a fish on the other line, I'll just slip the chain off and change it over. Won't take a minute."

"Youth and enthusiasm," Vady said as we walked out of earshot. "Those kids have it. Wife's as interested as he is. Living on that little boat, they've found real happiness."

"You knew that gurdy wouldn't work. Why didn't you tell him?"

"And spoil his fun? Of course it won't work. The first time they reel in the thing will melt like a Coney Island ice-cream cone. What if it does? Point is, they've worked and planned together."

"Poor kids," I said, "they've even bought bait. A forty-pound block."

"Sure. They'll go out thinking they have the world by the tail. They'll learn a lot of things they never dreamed of, but you can see they're stickers. They'll come in and rig up some other contraption and try again. Eventually they'll make a go of it."

"Imagine living on a little boat like that! So crowded, no place to take a bath, or wash, nothing to look at but water and sky and more boats."

"They have what everyone's striving for, social independence. That's what I like about Alaska. You can be your own man here."

"They'll be lucky to stay alive," I said, thinking of the sudden storms that sometimes whipped the waters of Tongass Narrows into a turmoil.

"We all have to die sooner or later, Babe. What difference does it make how we go? That's Alaska for you, a challenge. Adventure is what makes life worth living."

"No boats for me! I'll take my adventures out of books."

"With a boat there's no end to the places we could go. That's why I wanted to bring you up here, so I could show you the country. A small troller would be the thing. Just something to knock around in."

"Just one more thing to dispose of. The war won't last forever, and the less property we have the sooner we can sell it and get back home."

"A fellow ought to be able to pick up something good enough, if he knows how to fix it up."

Spring fishing hit the Coast Guard base like an epidemic. One of the boys bought a troller, fished in his free time, and made a few dollars. Immediately the sale of boats boomed. Our beach, with its long slope and the sand soft with sawdust washed in from the mill, was ideal for working on boats. Soon it resembled a shipyard.

Chief Monroe bought a hull and set it in a cradle near the house. A former boatbuilder and fisherman, the chief soon transformed his hull into a neat troller. Vady, at this time on night shore patrol, worked with him every available minute. I wondered how he could manage with so little sleep.

The chief was always immaculate. After a morning working on his boat he'd come in looking as if he'd just stepped out of the bath, donned a fresh uniform, and stopped by for a shave, haircut, and shine on the way.

When Vady came in after a morning's work, he sometimes looked as if he'd stumbled into the paint can or used himself for a brush.

Sleep or no sleep, I never saw Vady so contented. Truth is, I never saw much of him—just legs, or arms, or rear sticking out of some boat. I watched this activity with growing concern.

Then one day the inevitable happened. He came home looking as sheepish as a new father. "Guess what, Betsy! I put in a bid on a boat today. I think we'll get her! Won't that be swell?"

The boat, it developed, had been put up for sale to settle an estate. Vady's bid, three hundred dollars, was just half the appraised value. Surely, oh, surely someone else would bid higher.

Chapter 4

As long as Vady was so busy helping the boys with their boats, I dug out my paints, paper, and brushes. Maybe a new environment would solve the difficulties I'd had in Seattle. It did, to my delight, and I had a wonderful time. When I expected Vady home I'd gather up my things and get them out of sight. But his hours were irregular and sometimes he'd come in when I wasn't expecting him.

"You never have time for me any more," he complained one evening as he studied a picture I'd just completed. "All you do is paint."

"All you do is work on boats," I retorted.

"But I like boats," he protested. "I thought you liked them too."

"You like boats," I said firmly. "I like to paint."

"Paint, then, by all means," Vady said. "I only thought, now that the children are gone, we were going to do things together."

"Do you expect me to go out and work on the boats?"

"Oh, never mind!" he said. He shrugged his shoulders and walked out.

There followed a coolness between us that made us both unhappy. Everything went wrong. Again my paints and brushes would not respond. I couldn't settle down to anything. Vady was changed to duty that left his weekends free, but he was never home. If only we could get back to our old understanding, but there seemed no way to break through the barrier our little tiff had caused.

"We got the boat," he announced flatly one day. There was none of his usual exuberance. It was almost as if he didn't care.

If he didn't care, there was only one reason, and I knew what it was. He was right. It wasn't fun to do things alone.

"We did? Good!" I exclaimed, making it sound as if I meant it. "Where is it?"

Instantly the sparkle came back into his eyes. He jumped up, put his arms around me and kissed me. "You've been fooling Daddy," he gloated. "You wanted it as much as I did! She's out by the mill, tied to the boom logs. Come on!"

"Dirty-Face" O'Brian, the late owner, had lived aboard her for more years than anyone in Ketchikan could remember. She was dirty beyond belief. In the galley bits of musty food, old bones and torn papers, tin cans and rusted tools littered the floor. On the bunk a thin, mildewed mattress was heaped with a couple of greasy blankets and a moth-eaten overcoat. It was apparent that Dirty-Face hadn't been much of a housekeeper. The remains of his last meal stood in a rusty skillet on the tiny stove. He had been stricken suddenly.

My first glance had missed a partly filled case of rotten eggs, a pat of rancid butter, and a molded piece of bacon suspended from the ceiling by a string. All these decaying remnants and the odor of the bilge water, sloshing in the hold, sent me hurrying up the steep ladder to the deck and fresh air.

"How do you like her?" Vady asked happily.

"She's filthy!"

"She's dirty, all right," he admitted, "but just wait till I get her cleaned up. Did you notice her lines? She's steady as a tug. Chief Monroe says she has good possibilities, offered me five hundred dollars for her, in fact."

"Why didn't you take it?" I asked a little too eagerly.

"In a few weeks you wouldn't sell her for any money," he prophesied. "I'm going to build a pilothouse with two bunks in it. This summer we can spend our weekends fishing and exploring and live right on the boat. We'll have a grand time. She's had a hard life, but she'll make a dandy fishing boat."

We named her *Stinky*, uncouth but appropriate. While Vady cleaned and painted inside, I worked in the fresh air, painting the hull a brilliant green and lettering the name on her battered bow. When he began work on his wonderful pilothouse, it wouldn't come out square. Each day it looked more like a chicken coop balanced precariously on the trunk cabin. When I mentioned that it seemed a little out of line, he pointed out its advantages. Six large windows, and a sloping windshield!

"It does look a little queer," he had to admit at last,

"and it leaks. We'll cover it with canvas and paint it to match the deck, so it'll sort of blend in. The paint should make it waterproof."

We were a week covering it, stretching the canvas here, easing it there, pulling at wrinkles that wouldn't come out, quickly tacking it fast when we'd worked out a smooth spot. We covered the seams with wooden cleats, then painted, but the paint seeped away, leaving the canvas as porous as before.

"Paint it wet," Chief Monroe advised. "That'll fix it."

With hose in one hand and paintbrush in the other I followed his advice. When it dried, the paint had disappeared.

"Size it with glue," Mony said.

We sized it with glue. That night I propped my slacks against the outside wall, where they stood rigid until morning. The canvas was as scabby as a spawning salmon.

"Use flat white," said the chief.

We slapped on gallons of it, only to see it seep away like water through a sieve.

"Forget it," Vady said. "It doesn't rain so much in the summer, anyway. What say we take a run, wet a line, get a mess of fish."

I took my place in the chicken coop, my wings on the wheel, ready for the rattle and clank of the engine that would start our fishing trip.

The flywheel on the one-cylinder engine was as big as a washtub. It had to be turned over by hand, and it was a man-sized job. Vady pulled and strained, the engine coughed and sputtered. One last bone-breaking jerk and it started with a roar. Away we went down the channel, putt-putt-putt, at a breath-taking four knots.

I'd bought a surprise for Vady, a ship's log. It had looked so nautical in its red leather jacket with the gold lettering that I couldn't resist it. Now I took it from under the seat where I'd hidden it, and wrote boldly across the first page:

> 1:10 P.M. First fishing trip with *Stinky*. V sulking because B knocked new fishing hat into narrows with a rope. Purely accidental.
>
> 1:20 P.M. Passing Pennock Island. V feeling better. Must be the sunshine.

"What are you doing in there?" Vady called out. "Come out on deck. We're about to pass the *Sword Knot*."

"Not bad at all," I said. "We must be making good time to pass that big freighter—" I stopped short, for there was the *Sword Knot* coming toward us from the bow! I'd thought he meant we were overtaking her.

Vady came into the pilothouse and saw the handsome new log lying open beside the wheel.

"That's no way to make the entries," he said scornfully. "You have to keep the tides, winds and barometer readings under their proper headings. Put it away until later. Slow the motor to half speed while I put out the lines."

Back in the pilothouse, I sneaked in one more entry:

> 1:35 P.M. Wind: Not much. Tide: Going out, I guess.

That evening, after Vady had taken an aspirin and gone to bed with a wet towel on his head, I made my final entry for the day:

> 8:15 P.M. Home. Big salmon got away. Caught one red snapper. Motor stalled as we were coming in. Crank slipped. Asked V if he was hurt. When he yelled, "No, of course not!" I saw the bloody hole where the crank had knocked out a front tooth.

That was our first and last trip with *Stinky*. The very next week the war ended. Since Vady had been overage when he enlisted, his orders came through at once to report to Seattle for discharge.

"I suppose you'll be moving back to Seattle now," Chief Monroe said. "I'm stuck here for a while longer. My offer on *Stinky* still stands. She needs some work done on her, and it would give me something to kill time."

I waited anxiously for Vady's reply.

"No-o-o," he said at last, "I don't think I'm ready to sell. I figured Beth and I would take a little vacation. Do some fishing, see the country."

I tried to swallow my disappointment. After four years in the Service he was entitled to a vacation. A man had the worst of it, anyway, tied to a job the year round, handing over his pay check for food, clothes, rent, income tax this month, insurance next, nose to the grindstone, plod—plod—plod. If he wanted to take his vacation in Alaska, a couple of weeks, yes, even a month, I wouldn't stand in his way. Let him fish. Let him live off the land. Let him fly to the moon if he wanted to. I'd play along—for a month.

"I hope you won't have any trouble with the boat," Vady said as we stood on the wharf waiting for his ship to sail. "She leaks a little. You'll have to keep her pumped out."

It was nearly midnight that night when I was awakened by a resounding crash. I sat up in bed, startled and afraid. The wind wailed along the eaves, rain sloshed against the windows and ran down like liquid rickrack. Waves slapped against the wanigan, pushed one another along the side, and died with a hiss in the sand.

The wanigan trembled again as something struck against it. I jumped up and ran to the window. There, riding high on the dark, stormy water was the hulking outline of *Stinky*, up to the porch in her cradle. In the gloom she looked as big and menacing as a sperm whale. With every wave she rose higher and higher as she lunged at her mooring lines.

What could I do? It would be impossible to move her, yet it seemed certain the cradle would break up. The noise was terrific, wind howling, the wanigan creaking and groaning, the rain skittering across the roof and the bang and crash of the cradle each time it hit the porch.

I dressed hurriedly, ready to run in case a giant wave should catapult the boat right through the walls and into the living room.

Then I waited. I walked the floor. Afraid to look out the window. Afraid not to. At last, after what seemed like hours, I knew the tide had turned. The boat was settling. Two hours later, when the tide had run out, she stood upright on the sand.

Things always went wrong when Vady was away, I thought, as I crawled back into the cold bed to wait for daylight.

Vady's remark that she leaked a little didn't half describe it. I found that out in the morning when I went out to pump and found the bilge half full of oily water. That bilge! It held more water than the city reservoir! After an hour of futile effort with the pump, I gave up. Nothing for it but to bail, and that I did for the next two hours. Balanced shakily on the edge of the hatch, I lowered a five-gallon pail on the end of a rope, jiggled it until it fell over on its side and filled up, then pulled it up hand over hand and dumped it. It was a gamble each time, would I pull up the pail, or would the pail pull me down?

At last the bilge was dry, and although my back felt as if someone had been jumping on me for the last two hours, I had an inner glow of satisfaction to think I had handled the situation so nicely by myself. I'd take another look around to see that everything was hunky-dory for the night. As I squeezed in between the cradle and the house I found that everything was far from all right. The inside of the cradle was badly battered, with nails bristling out of it like porcupine quills and broken boards pointing splintery fingers at me. Another windy night would finish the cradle entirely, and *Stinky* too, without a doubt.

I telephoned Chief Monroe. He came out at high tide, looking spruce and efficient, bringing three Coast Guard boys with him. After considerable effort they managed to get the boat into the cradle where the chief had kept his own boat.

That night I went to bed assured that everything would be all right. Let it rain! Let it blow! Chief Monroe knew how to take care of boats.

In the morning when I went out to bail, bent almost double from yesterday's efforts, I stopped short in dismay!

Water poured in a thin stream from beneath *Stinky*'s stern! It dripped from gaping cracks along the whole length of the hull. It splashed softly on the rocks and dribbled away in the sand.

As I walked around the bow I saw that one of her planks had been broken and stuck out at a crazy angle. A yawning hole, where she had settled on a rock, had opened up in her bottom.

She hadn't been a dream boat at best. Now she was a wreck. How could I tell Vady when he came home?

Although I didn't have any hopes that Mony could save her, I called him again.

"She'll need a good deal of work," he said, shaking his head at the sight of her. "We can put on a wet patch to keep the water out, but she'll have to have several new planks."

That afternoon, as we raced with the tide, I learned how to make a wet patch, an art I'd never expected to have any use for. A wet patch is a messy thing. We laid a large piece of canvas on the beach, then, because we were short of tar, smeared it with all the odds and ends of paint we had. Gooey gobs of white, red, and green paint and blobs of black tar would make it waterproof. Mony finished tacking it to the hull with wooden strips just as the tide reached us.

When Vady came home, ten days later, I could hardly bring myself to tell him about the boat. I put it off as long as possible. Thinking a full stomach would be a good shock absorber, I took him to the kitchen with me while I prepared dinner.

"You're a free man again," I said, turning up the oil in the range. "How does it seem to be a civilian?"

Vady threw his leg over a chair and sat down with his arms around the back. "I don't quite know. I can't realize it yet. I keep expecting the phone to ring and orders to report for duty."

"It's going to take a little while to get used to seeing you in anything but navy blue. Tell me about the States. Was it good to get home? Didn't you hate to come back?"

"It was terrible! A regular madhouse! You've no idea how things have changed down there. It was rush, rush, rush from morning until night. Strained faces, everyone griping about rationing, points, and shortages. We just didn't know how lucky we were, living in a war zone through most of the war. And the traffic! After the pace we're used to, it was like a crowd at a Joe Louis fight. I never saw so much determination in so many people! Pushing and shoving and walking all over you. I don't see how they stand it!"

"Softy," I laughed. "We'll soon get used to it. We've

just slowed down without realizing it. We're lucky you have your civil-service job to go back to."

"Oh no, Babe!" Vady said emphatically. "I'm not going back to that! I never hated anything so much in my life."

Now what? I'd felt so secure, thinking he'd take up right where he left off, and he'd been promoted just at the last. I'd even indulged in a little dreaming about how it would be—more income, and fewer expenses with the children on their own.

He jumped up to walk nervously back and forth. "Do you remember old Otto, the miner?" he asked at last. "The one who said, 'You neffer get nowheres, poys, so long as you vork by de vistle?' He was right. No more vistle."

"You mean you aren't going to work any more?"

"Don't look so alarmed, Babe. I'm just not going to work for the other fellow. Why should I tie myself to a job just to earn a measly living? Life's too short at best. I'm going to enjoy it while I can."

"Everybody works."

"Who's everybody? That's your trouble, Dolly. You're in a rut. You think because Smith and Jones and Brackenstrop have jobs, Eberhart has to have one. That's what makes people old—stale lives, stale thoughts, stagnation. As soon as a fellow loses his imagination and is afraid to take a chance, he's through. Life is a series of phases: Youth, when you think you know all the answers; marriage, and the years of bringing up a family, when you find you don't know anything after all; then . . ."

"Grandparents!" I cut in. "When you quit work and retire on nothing. I wonder what the children will think when they find out Grandpa's on strike."

"What difference does it make what they think? Do we tell them how to run their lives? That phase is over. We don't have to be good examples any more."

"At our age we should be thinking about security."

"Good Lord, Babe! If I'd let you, you'd settle down in one spot and never move. Well, I won't let you. Why all the stress on security? Do you think I'm too old to make a living for two?"

"No-o-o," I said, "but there were a few times when you were younger . . . Remember the year—"

"Don't bother," Vady interrupted quickly. "It's different now. We haven't scratched the surface." He walked over to the window and looked out. "What do you know? I've been home all this time and haven't even been out to see the boat!"

The time had come. "I wrecked your boat and spoiled your vacation," I said, then quickly went on with the whole miserable story.

"It wasn't your fault," he said when I had finished. "We'll have to make other plans. I'll sell her to Mony."

"Oh, he'd never buy her now, not after seeing that hole in her bottom!"

But Vady was right and I was wrong. The chief did buy her for four hundred fifty dollars!

"I can patch her up," he said. "Put in some new planks and patch the keel with lead. With a new paint job it won't show. There's nothing wrong with her, except she's rotten through and through. The bottom's so full of dry rot she's soft as a rubber ball. When she settled on that rock, all the seams opened up, but as soon as the pressure was off she flopped back into shape again. She'll last a season or two. I can easily sell her to some sucker from the States."

The next day the chief towed her away to a grid downtown. Walking by shortly afterward, I saw a group of small boys watching something on the beach below. I walked over to the railing and looked down. There was *Stinky*, and in her hold was Chief Monroe, bailing with a five-gallon pail.

For once the chief was ruffled. His hair hung damply against his cheeks. His shirt clung lovingly to arms and back. His pants cuffs dripped dirty water over his sodden shoes.

"Hi, mister, does your boat leak?" yelled one of the kids.

No answer from below.

"Say," shouted another, "what's the name of your boat?"

"S-T-I-N-K-Y," spelled the first boy. "Sounds like Stinky. Is that a name? A boat name?"

I backed away from the rail and went on. This was no time to talk to Chief Monroe.

The next time I saw the boat there was a large piece of plywood nailed over the letters I had designed with such care.

Before he'd had her a month he sold her for six hundred fifty dollars!

"Not much profit," I said when Vady told me.

"Pretty good, I'd say. He cleared about a hundred and fifty on her, not counting his time. Gave him something to do while he's waiting for his discharge."

One day a "Coastie" hailed Vady on the street with, "Say, Chief, there's a boat down at the basin that's just what you're looking for. She's small, but roomy, and rigged for trolling. She's got a pilothouse that's all skedaddled, but you could tear that off easy enough and build another. She's got a new paint job, and she's a bargain at the price."

"Sounds worth looking into," Vady said.

"*My Chance*, on Float E," the boy called after us.

Vady's "Hello, down there," brought a pale, skinny youth up from below. His respectful "Hi, Chief," told me that he was a recently discharged Coast Guardsman. Vady greeted him warmly with, "Hello there, Johnny."

A robust Indian woman of uncertain age had followed Johnny to the door, then, seeing us, retreated.

"My boat? She's not for sale!" Johnny said, and there was the pride of ownership in his voice. "I just bought her myself. She was cheaper than a house. A fellow can't rent a place in this damned town, but you can't go wrong on a deal like this. Look't them windows. Ain't they dandy? Wife's makin' curtains for 'em now. Where else could you get good, roomy livin' quarters and a fishin' boat all at the same time? And dirt cheap. Only a thousand dollars."

She didn't look like the same boat, painted white with green trim. It was only by looking closely at the faint discoloration under the name that one could see the letters, "S-T-I-."

Whenever Vady was away I worked at my painting. Alaska was a challenge, the scenery so different from anything else I'd tried. Could I make people feel the density of the forests, the depth and coldness of the water, the ruthlessness of the land and sea deceptively veiled in beauty?

Finally I finished several pictures that partly satisfied me. I put them on display in a downtown window and soon had more orders than I could fill.

One blustery day in November, Vady had gone to town early. I had just turned on the lights for evening when I heard his step on the porch. He bounded in with a rush of cold air.

"Where's my housykeep?" he shouted. "I have a surprise for you! A Christmas present! You'll never guess."

I didn't need to guess. Only one thing could make him look like that.

"A boat?" I asked fearfully.

"That's it, Babe! How'd you know? A troller! A real fishing boat!"

Chapter 5

"You aren't going to see this boat until I have her shipshape," Vady told me, thinking of my dismay when I first saw *Stinky*.

"Good idea," I agreed. "Just tell me about her. Is she as large as *Stinky?* As old as the teakwood boat? How wide? How long? What color? How about the kitchen and the beds?"

"Betsy," Vady said reprovingly, "please learn to speak in more nautical terms. She's beamy, not wide. There's a bunk, no beds. I think you'll find the galley adequate. There's no kitchen."

"Aye, aye, Cap," I said, giving him a proper salute.

"She has a capacity of eight tons, and is Diesel-powered. It's the best fuel there is, safe, reliable, and economical. The oil line goes to the cookstove, too."

"An oil range!" I marveled. "She must be pretty nice at that, luxurious, even."

Visions of something between a cruiser and the *Prince George*, the ship that had brought us to Ketchikan, went through my mind.

"Well, maybe not quite that," Vady laughed, "but you'll like her."

For two weeks I saw very little of my husband. He was gone early and late, coming home at night paint-flecked, tired, and beaming, only to be up at daylight the next morning to catch the first bus to town.

One day I found him on the back porch, whistling blithely as he worked over a strange-looking three-sided box.

"What *are* you doing?" I asked. "Don't you know that's the extra leaf to the dining table you're cutting up?"

"Right size for a top, exactly," he said, grinning as he finished his cut and one end of the leaf dropped to the floor. "Nice hardwood, too. You won't need extra leaves for the table where you're going, but you'll need this. None of those deck-bucket deals for us."

I forgave him later when I found how necessary his contrivance was. Well camouflaged, with its leafy top, it served its purpose during the day, tucked into an obscure corner by the engine. At night it fitted snugly into the pilothouse. Chance visitors aboard used it as a stool, unaware that they were sitting on our head.

All too soon for me came the day when Vady announced the *Emblem* was ready for her trial run. Lockers well stocked with provisions and two tons of ice in the hold, he brought her home and tied her to the float.

"Tomorrow," he said with that night-before-Christmas

look on his face, "we'll be ready to go. We'll make a trip around Revillagigedo Island and take in—"

"Wait. Where's that?"

I was astonished when he told me. We'd been in Ketchikan more than a year and I'd thought all the time the name of the island we were on was Revilla. Few people try to stumble through the full Spanish original, Revillagigedo.

"February seems early in the year for sight-seeing," I suggested hopefully.

"Perhaps, but we want to try her out, don't we? Besides, we might find some fish. This is the beginning of our program. Our dream about to come true. You won't have a thing to do"—he paused, seeing my doubtful expression, then hurried on—"nothing, that is, but order the crew around and steer the boat. Take your paints. There's lots of room on deck. We'll set your easel up and you can paint all day."

His sudden about-face left me speechless. Somehow I couldn't imagine painting at an easel set up on the deck of a troller, in February or any other time.

We were about to live his dream and in his usual generous way he was giving me back mine.

The *Emblem* was built in the days when a troller was built for one purpose—to fish. Not much thought was given to the fisherman's comfort. Most of the room was for fish storage, for in those days the fishermen iced their fish. With the advent of buying scows on the grounds, day fishing has become the rule, rather than the exception, with the boats selling to some scow at night.

Each year more and more wives, and often whole families, go along for a summer's outing. Trollers are improving accordingly. Two-way radios, fathometers, automatic pilots, and electric gurdies make for greater safety, while inside heads, showers, refrigerators, and cute little ranges, all white enamel, fool the wives into thinking that housekeeping on a boat will be a cinch. But the *Emblem* was built in 1919.

When Vady said the galley was adequate, he meant just that. There was room for a stove, sink, bunk, and food lockers. We sat on our groceries, which were stored under the seat that ran along one side. The door to the cupboard where we kept dishes and cutlery let down to make a table. The bunk, about three-quarter-bed size at the head, narrowed toward the bow to about eighteen inches, which kept us playing "footsies" all night as each struggled for room to stretch out. Once we were installed there was one vacant space left, a little strip of wall above the bunk, just long enough to hang the guns. To say there was room for us is stretching a point. We pivoted on each other's elbows, walked on each other's feet, and the bunk was as hard to get out of as a fish trap. I marveled every morning when, after a terrific struggle, we were ready for the day each dressed in his own clothes.

The big old Diesel motor squatted at one end of the galley; the fresh-water tank filled the bow, with all but the head of the bunk over it.

But the afterdeck! That was something else again; it was as large as some cabaret dance floors. The raised hatch was set well back, but there was still room for four fish checkers and a large cockpit. The little skiff fitted easily along one side of the hatch; the passageway to the cockpit was on the other side.

From the beginning my place was in the pilothouse. "You may as well learn to steer," Vady said. "It saves a fisherman a lot of time if he doesn't have to watch where he's going and steer from the cockpit. From now on you're the captain, I'm the crew.

"Steering a boat's no trick. You just point her nose at something, and after a while you're there."

"Umn-hu?"

It was a beautiful morning. The *Emblem* made better time, with less fuss, than *Stinky* had. Soon we could see Guard Island, with the lighthouse looming tall and white in the distance, marking the crossroads of the waterways. To the left, on the westward, was Clarence Strait, leading in from Dixon Entrance and the Pacific Ocean. To the right Behm Canal began its enfolding circle of Revillagigedo Island. Behind a sheltering chain of small islands Clover Passage would take us five miles on our way through protected waters.

Vady called from the cockpit, "Slow down to half speed. I'm going to put out the lines."

We crawled through the pass, then slipped between two islands into Behm Canal, where a heavy ground swell was running. Nothing had happened; the lines trailed slackly behind. Then all at once I saw a pole bobbing!

"Fish on!" I cried excitedly. "Hurry, he'll get away!"

"It's nothing to get excited about," Vady said, fumbling and shaking and knocking over the spoon bucket in his haste. "All in a day's work," he said, starting the gurdy and catching his glove in the line. The glove pulled off and wound around the block. "Damn it!" he exploded, stopping the rattling gurdy and yanking away at the glove in a frenzy.

"Easy does it," I cautioned as he freed the glove and started the gurdy again. "Don't get excited."

I left the wheel and ran on deck.

"D-d-don't leave the wheel," Vady yelled, "she'll turn around and langle the tines."

He unsnapped the first leader, reached out for the next,

and then we saw our fish—but no! What was this? It came over the side battered and bloody, bitten off halfway between its head and its tail. What deep-sea robber had beaten us to our prize? We'd caught our first half fish!

The wind had increased and was kicking up a sizable slop. I was wondering where we'd spend the night, when Vady began to pull the lines. The early winter dusk was already blurring the shore line. I was glad to turn the boat over to the mate. After studying the chart he turned into a little cove at the mouth of a creek and dropped anchor.

"Isn't this swell?" he asked as we lingered over our half-a-salmon supper. "You like it, don't you, Babe?"

"It's so small . . ." I began doubtfully. "I don't see how we'll manage a whole season."

"Small!" he echoed. "What would you do with any more room? We have everything we need right here."

To Vady there's no such thing as cramped quarters. Small places may be "cozy" or "snug" but never cramped. Should I tell him that to me it was like living in a cave? That every time I took a deep breath I felt as if I was robbing his lungs to fill my own? But why spoil his pleasure?

"Do fishermen always get so excited when they catch a fish?" I asked him.

"I wasn't excited." Vady's denial was somewhat shamefaced, but he had the nerve to look me in the eye. "I was only trying to hurry, as you told me."

Next morning, after breakfast, Vady pointed out our day's fishing grounds on the chart. A feeling of inadequacy came over me as he showed me the dotted lines marking a shoal and told me that I'd have to watch closely to keep outside of it. How could anyone watch for something that wasn't there, for there were no dotted lines on the rough waters ahead. Worse yet, that wavering line enclosed a pock-marked section of chart, studded with the stars and dots that mean big rocks and little rocks to chart makers. I knew the chart was going to bring me trouble, just as I knew it all summer, but I forgot my uneasiness when I saw a bobbing pole.

"Fish! You've got a fish on every line! Look at those poles!"

But Vady wasn't fooled. "Bottom!" he yelled. "We're on bottom! Speed up and head for deep water!"

Being the captain in this case didn't signify that I was in command. The crew was the law. I speeded up and, looking back, saw that the poles had ceased their samba and the lines were streaming straight out behind, the weights hurdling the waves.

So this was fishing! A wobbling pole didn't always mean fish. Sometimes it meant the loss of spoons and expensive gear. We had been lucky this time. We had lost only two hooks.

We found a good moorage that night. Three miles inside a bay where there was a deserted mining claim with a small cabin on the beach and a float offshore, to which we tied. Vady put out the crab trap and dropped a hand line over the side.

Later, while the engineer oiled up, I got out our copy of *Knight's Modern Seamanship* to "salt" my vocabulary. "Beam-ends," I read, "said of a vessel when she is hove over or listed until her deck beams approach the vertical." I hoped I'd never have occasion to use the term. "Bitter end: the last part of a rope or the last link in an anchor chain." "Cow's tail: the frayed or untidy end of a rope." "Dead rope: a rope not led through a block or sheave." "Long-legged: a deep-draft vessel."

When Vady pulled the hand line our supper was assured—a wriggling rock cod flapped on deck. The trap yielded a crab. Perhaps this fellow Riley had something after all.

Stormbound in the morning, we stood on deck watching the waves beat against the rocks onshore. A deer came out of the woods and picked its way daintily to a jutting ledge, surveying its domain. For a while it watched us, unafraid, then, its curiosity satisfied, disappeared into the deep woods. I turned to go below, when Vady stopped me with a hand on my arm and pointed to three land otters playing in the water close by. They paid no attention to us, but went on with their games, diving and reappearing, chasing one another round and round or stretching their long, thick necks high out of the water as if they were standing on tiptoe. Finally they swam to the beach and crawled out on a log, where they rolled and tumbled like playful kittens, scratched their thick fur with their hind feet, and rubbed their chins on the rough bark of the log.

"They don't dive at all like seals," I whispered. "First their head goes down, then their round rump, then that final flip of the tail. Seals always look as if something under them had pulled them down."

The otters had heard me. With a mass dive they were gone.

"Isn't that worth the whole trip?" Vady asked. "There's something so thrilling about seeing wild things. It must have been like this in the Garden of Eden, before wild animals were afraid of men." He picked up a handful of spoons and went jingling down to the galley.

"Don't tell me you're going to polish those," I said as he began to drag out rags and Brilliantshine. "We've only caught half a fish. Some of those spoons haven't even been in the water."

"Spoons always need polishing," Vady said with dignity.

He was right. They always do.

"It doesn't make sense," I said. "Spoons have to be polished when they aren't used, and this galley is dirty already. I can't understand it."

I could see it wasn't going to be easy to live up to my boast that we'd have the cleanest boat in the fishing fleet. Our oil stove was behaving badly, refusing to generate, allowing the oil to overflow the pot at frequent intervals. Then we would have to turn it off and let the extra oil burn out. Not only that; we left a trail of oily soot wherever we went. It covered the deck, blew into the pilothouse, tracked into the galley. Our shoes, hands, and faces were speckled with it. Vady used strong language, while I scrubbed everything in sight. The final result was a smeared gray coating over everything I'd washed, including ourselves.

"I can't do anything about it until we get in," Vady said at last.

Later in the day he put out the crab trap again and that evening we feasted on the three huge crabs he caught. It seemed only a few minutes after we had turned in that I felt him twisting and jerking, trying to free himself from the tiny wedge that was his share of the bunk.

"What goes on?" I asked sleepily.

"I'm going to get up and start the fire. It's time to get going."

I rolled over and looked at the clock.

"Did Riley get up at five o'clock?" I groaned. "It won't be light for a couple of hours at least."

"You don't have to get up, Dolly," my husband said soothingly. "Sleep as long as you like. I'll get breakfast."

I pulled the covers up and settled down for a nice, long

nap, with the whole three-quarter bunk to myself. How kind and thoughtful he was!

"What was that?" I jumped up as I heard a fiendish yell.

"Br-r-r! I just stepped outside. It's colder than Billy-be-damned. I didn't mean to wake you. Go back to sleep."

I settled down again.

There was a clattering thump. The cupboard door flew open and the coffeepot hit the floor with a bang.

I pulled the covers over my ears.

My husband began to sing. Darn those people who wake up so happy they have to sing before the coffee is ready!

"Where in the heck do you keep the pancake flour?"

"That does it," I sighed, and crawled out of the bunk.

The water was still choppy as we left the shelter of the bay. I was dreading the prospects of a rough ride, when I saw a school of porpoises coming toward us. On they came, rolling to the surface in a spray of white water, looping under and up again, nearer and nearer, straight for the boat. Then they were all around us, darting under the bow, streaking along beside us, or cutting through the water with a sudden flash of their white bellies. We learned, during the summer, that we could always count on them in rough weather. There was something about the *Emblem* that seemed to fascinate them. Sometimes there would be as many as five schools coming at us from as many different directions, following us for hours, playing around the boat. On quiet days they seldom came near, but rolled lazily about in the distance singly or in pairs, as if enjoying the calm water.

Watching them, I forgot to be afraid, and before I knew it we were docking at Bell Island, one of the natural wonder spots of Alaska. There are no fuel problems at the Bell Island Resort, for the buildings are heated throughout by water piped in from the hot springs. It has everything vacationers could desire—hot springs, mineral springs, an icy-cold mountain stream babbling past the resort and the neat little cabins, fresh-water fishing, salt-water fishing and hunting, all within easy reach.

That night a troller tied to the dock beside us.

Vady went visiting. The fisherman had been fishing here several days without results. He grudgingly gave out the information that it was still too early, the fish hadn't come in yet. Vady's spirits somewhat dampened by the cool reception, he suggested that the rest of our trip should be a sight-seeing cruise only, taking in the wonderful sights of Walker Cove and Rudyerd Bay, which, we had been told, rival in beauty the fjords of Norway.

Although we awoke to a blinding snowstorm, we headed out into it. By this time I considered myself quite a navigator. Hadn't I eased up to the float last night with hardly a jar? And hadn't I been able to keep my balance during the worst of the blows—by taking a firm grip on the wheel with one hand and clinging to the window ledge with the other?

The snow, falling in great fluffy flakes, stuck to the window in a solid mass, in spite of the frequent trips to the bow Vady made to scrape it from the outside of the window. Soon our destination, across the channel, was blotted out entirely.

"We'll have to go back to Bell Island," I said thankfully, thinking of the safe wharf to tie to.

"Nonsense!" scoffed the crew, setting me back on my heels. "Why do you think we have a compass and charts?"

Hardly a fair question, I thought. I'd already found that the chart was very useful for picking out likely anchorages, rocks, and shoals. As for the compass, I hadn't thought much about it. Boats carried compasses, and they gave a nice, nautical touch to the pilothouse. Heretofore we'd always been able to see our goal. What if we did go straight out to sea one minute and toward land the next? We always got there.

Patiently Vady showed me the lubber line on the compass, telling me to keep the course figure beneath it. "A good navigator never deviates," he explained, "not even half a degree either way. You have to learn to catch her before she swings."

This was something else again; with the tides and wind combining to swing the bow first this way and then that, I was to catch her before she swung! While I was busy trying to master the new technique the engine coughed and died!

"Fuel tank dry!" called the engineer from below. Instantly I had visions of drifting, perhaps for days, until some stray boat chanced by. Why, oh why, had we ever come? Or at least why hadn't we chosen some more traveled route? My reading had included several accounts of boats adrift at sea. Some had run out of food. They had all been rescued only after grueling experiences.

The familiar chug of the Diesel brought me out of my morbid reveries. It had never occurred to me that there was more fuel. Gallons of it, hidden in those secret recesses below deck. It was necessary only to turn a tap to let it into the empty tank.

In spite of our erratic course our little cove finally emerged from its screen of snow. "I don't see how you ever did it," I told Vady admiringly.

Later, as we sat in the warm galley swinging safely at anchor, proud of our evening's catch of eleven large crabs, I thought how pleasant a fishing trip would be if I could only lose my fear of the water. Lucky for me I couldn't see too far into the future.

"Let's take a look at the map, pick out a tie-up for tomorrow night, write up the diary, and get to bed."

Vady grabbed his head in both hands. "Babe! What kind of talk is that? Chart, anchorage, log, sack down—remember?"

In the morning six inches of soot-spotted snow covered the decks. Lines and rigging trailed white festoons overhead. The snow came down faster as we headed south, down the east side of Revillagigedo Island. Keeping as close to the shore line as safely possible and using it as our guide, we reached Walker Cove just as the waves began breaking over the bow. A short distance inside the water was calm and the skies lightened enough for us to enjoy the grandeur of that beautiful fjord.

For five miles we wound our way between precipitous granite cliffs. Small avalanches rumbled down the mountains on either side, and great chunks of hard-packed snow drifted by. At last, rounding a point, we came into a peaceful little harbor at the mouth of a creek. The tide flats, washed clean of snow, seemed to hold out welcoming arms. Three eagles circled slowly overhead, and a pair of white swans, whiter than the snow itself, floated gracefully in the creek. Frightened by the boat, they lifted their heavy bodies and with a great flapping of wings set off for a more secluded spot.

We put the skiff in the water and went ashore for clams. We found neither the littleneck nor butter clams we had found on other beaches, but a soft-shelled variety that made an excellent chowder after we had discarded their tough black necks.

"What a wonderful place to sleep!" I murmured as we settled down for the night, but our rest was short.

Foolishly we left a fire in the stove, as the galley got so cold and damp during the night. At five I wakened with a start, gasping and choking for breath! The place was filled with smoke!

I jumped out of the bunk and, groping around in the dark, found the oil valve on the stove and shut it off. The pot was full of oil! Suddenly it ignited. Flames shot out in all directions! The whole stove seemed ablaze!

"Grab the fire extinguisher!" Vady yelled. "Get one out of the pilothouse! Stand ready now! If the oil drips out anywhere we'll throw something over it. Look outside and see if the deck's on fire!"

It wasn't, but the stovepipe was an awesome sight. Red from top to bottom, with black smoke rolling out in billows, and flames licking through it.

The bulkhead began to smoke. "How do you use this darned thing?" I chattered, shaking from cold and fright.

"Wait! Not yet," Vady said, "hold it! Hold it! The flames seem to be dying down. It'll burn itself out."

I'm sure that, as we stood there watching, we both had the same thought: How far could we row in our cranky little skiff before we swamped?

As the stove gradually cooled, Vady made a welcome suggestion.

"What say we go home as soon as it's light enough to see? I wouldn't trust a fire in that old stove again."

We crawled back into the bunk to keep warm. Then at first faint hint of dawn we breakfasted on a can of cold beans, pulled the anchor, and headed out. The wind had died during the night, but the snow still fell. It even lay on the water, a blanket of greenish slush. We seemed to be in a different world, a world without motion, direction or distance; a world of distorted perspectives, where we were stationary and objects came to us out of the gloom.

Gulls loomed by with startling suddenness; bits of driftwood assumed the size of saw logs; a shadow on the water looked like a towering wave, and as I turned to take it on the bow, it disappeared into nothingness.

I was just enjoying the utter calm, when the water was darkened by a sudden gust of wind. Another followed, kicking up tiny waves. In less than ten minutes we were pounding into white-crested fury as a sudden squall swept down upon us.

"Vady!" I called. "I'm scared to death. This is awful! Can't you do something?"

He came up from the galley on the run, and after a glance at the chart took over the wheel. He was as clever as Houdini, I thought, as he squeezed the *Emblem* into a tiny bight on a nearby island that looked to me too narrow to enter. Putting the skiff over the side, he rowed to shore and fastened shore lines to trees on either side of the bight.

"Now we're as safe as if we were tied in our own back yard," he said as he pulled the skiff back aboard and secured it.

I wasn't so sure. Not with those williwaws striking us, first on one side and then on the other, and the *Emblem* heeling over with every furious gust. Not after seeing a wind of such force make up in a matter of minutes.

"What if we'd been out where there was no island?" I asked him, amazed that he could take the storm so lightly.

"We weren't in any danger. There are always bays and harbors to run to. It might be uncomfortable for a while, but there's seldom a time when an hour's run wouldn't take us to shelter."

An hour! A person could die a thousand deaths in an

hour! Without a fire it was cold and miserable in the galley. Oh, for a cup of scalding coffee!

In another hour the wind had shifted to the north and was blowing straight into the bight.

Vady took in the shore lines. We backed carefully out and headed for Point Alava. Remembering it as we had seen it from the sturdy decks of the *Prince George* on our way north, I'd been dreading Alava ever since Vady had mentioned going around the island. Out into the unprotected ocean we went, with the wild waters beating against barren cliffs close by.

Even my imagination left me unprepared for what we faced. Those mountainous waves seemed beyond measurement. Great gray swells rolled endlessly. The *Emblem,* her Diesel laboring mightily, climbed to the top of a wave, hung balanced for a moment on the crest, then with a sickening lurch slid into the trough. Down, down, only to face another wall of gray water. If only there hadn't been so much noise—the roar of the water, the slap of the waves, the rigging snapping and groaning! Down in the galley pots and pans fell from the cupboard, making it impossible for us to hear each other talk.

The next two hours seemed like a lifetime as we watched the waves breaking on the rocky shore, drenching the very treetops with foam. Then the swells began to subside as we approached the more sheltered waters leading to Tongass Narrows.

Twenty miles from home! Earlier in the day that would have seemed like an endless distance, but now home seemed close, and, oh, so desirable.

As the familiar buoy lights of the narrows came in sight, Vady went below to make some sandwiches. Relieved now that the worst was over, I even managed a few snatches of song. We'd made it! Our trial trip was run!

The lights of Ketchikan were like a greeting from an old friend. For once the rising wind was of no importance. I had seen too many winds in Tongass Narrows to be frightened of a squall in our own back yard.

We were home! Swinging in around the end of the mill to tie to the float, I whirled the wheel with all my strength to turn the *Emblem* back out into the channel. We had nearly hit a raft of logs that had been moved in by the mill during our absence and was blocking the entrance!

"What are you doing?" Vady called from below.

"You'll have to take over. We can't reach the float."

"I'll just run up to the boom," he said, taking in the situation, "let you out in the skiff, and take the boat back to Thomas Basin. It's blowing up and she'll be safer down there. You don't mind rowing to the house, do you?"

Mind? To our own comfortable, warm house? Hardly!

It took a few minutes to get the *Emblem* back to the boom. Then, leaving me at the wheel, he scrambled over onto the logs with the bow line in his hand.

No sooner was I alone than a gust of wind swept the boat out again into the narrows, with Vady clinging desperately to the line. The *Emblem* was a heavy boat. It took all his strength to hold her.

Reason gave way to panic as I reached down in the dark for the shift, thinking to go ahead slowly and ease the strain on the line. In my haste I grabbed the throttle instead and gave it a jerk that killed the engine!

I jumped for the door and ran on deck. Vady would have to tell me how to start the motor. He was teetering dangerously on his unstable perch. Then, as I opened my mouth to call to him, the boat gave a roll, the line tightened, and he plunged into the icy waters of Tongass Narrows!

Stifling a scream, I dashed below, wild thoughts racing through my head. I was alone on the *Emblem* with a stalled motor! And Vady! I hadn't waited to see him come up after his plunge. What if he had hit his head on a log as he went down? Even now he might be out there unconscious, drowning! The tide was running out. Was the *Emblem* drifting with it?

I reached for the handle that had always started the motor with ease—for Vady. Ouch! I jerked my hand away from the hot exhaust pipe and reached to the right—to the left. Finding the handle at last, I gave it a tug. It didn't move. I tried again, harder, then up and down, from side to side. I couldn't budge it.

Tides sometimes had undertows that carried men out to sea. Even strong swimmers were often powerless against them. I gave the handle another jerk—to no avail.

With a sob of frustration I gave it up and ran back on deck. At first I couldn't make Vady out in the early winter dusk, then I saw him astraddle the logs, his feet still dangling in the water, with the rope taut in his hand. He looked up and shouted at me, "Come ahead! Slowly!"

"I can't! Motor's dead!" I yelled back.

At that he began inching slowly forward, his hands groping over the logs, searching for something—anything to tie to. At last he found it. Two logs joined by a short chain. He made the rope fast, then, straightening carefully, got to his feet. Even with the *Emblem* secured it took him some time to work it over to the logs inch by inch to get aboard.

"Why in heck didn't you start the motor?" he said.

"The handle wouldn't turn."

"Did you unfasten it?"

Some captain! I hadn't even known it was fastened!

"Come below," Vady said shortly.

Right then, from a very wet instructor, I learned a valuable lesson, how to unfasten that blamed handle and start the motor.

That important matter taken care of, Vady put the skiff over the side and I rowed home while he took the boat back to the basin. No house ever looked more wonderful! We lived in a palace! We could pass each other without touching. There were heat, hot water, and a tub to use it in.

Later, when Vady came home, cold and soggy, he could still laugh. "Why didn't you use some of those new words you learned? That sure was the bitter end I had out there tonight."

As I crawled into bed, I made a resolution. My fishing days were over forever! He'd never talk me into leaving home again.

Chapter 6

Vady didn't mention making another trip at once. There were several changes he wanted to make on the gear. I was thankful to put off telling him, for the time being, that I'd made up my mind to stay home.

He called me on the phone one afternoon. He'd been talking to a fellow who had a piano on his boat. A piano, mind you! I just had to come down and see it. "Shut the oven off. To heck with your pie. You don't get a chance to see something like this every day," Vady insisted.

She was a beautiful boat, modern in every respect. The galley, built on deck, had a nine-by-twelve rug on the floor, a white enamel range, built-in breakfast nook, and a davenport that opened up to make a bed. Below there were four bunks, a roomy closet, lockers for food, and a head with a shower.

His wife played the guitar, the fisherman played the piano, and they both sang. All very nice in port, but I couldn't help wondering who made the music in places like Point Alava, for instance.

After I'd ohd and ahd enough to please my husband, we took a sight-seeing trip along the floats.

"Play a game," Vady said. "I'd like to get some old-timer to show me how to choke herring."

"Why? You've been around the trollers enough, you surely ought to know."

"New methods. New times. There's always new things to learn."

"Fishermen won't talk. You know that."

"It's just a matter of finding the right bird," Vady said.

"What's the game?" I asked, curious, but rather fearful, too. His games didn't always turn out to my advantage. I remembered only too well a couple of times in the States when he'd "played a game."

One time we had been Christmas shopping in Seattle. At the Public Market a Japanese woman had a display of poinsettias on the floor in front of her stand. While her back was turned, Vady picked up one of the pots of flowers, stuck it under my arm, and, taking my elbow, led me firmly away. Turmoil broke loose! The little Japanese rushed out screaming, "Thief! Thief!" knocking over several pots in her haste. Passers-by stopped to stare.

"Shame on you!" Vady said, to my horror. "Give me those flowers, woman!"

He snatched them from me, took them back, and set them carefully on the floor.

"My wife wanted them for my grave," he said, "but you see I didn't die."

He tipped his hat and walked away, while the poor little Japanese lady, straightening up her stand, screamed after him, "You make too much joke!"

The other "game" took place in a small town where we had gone to a Fourth-of-July band concert. I had broken my leg earlier in the year and was just getting around on crutches with my leg still in a cast. After a day of celebrating I was badly disheveled.

When the musicians came down off the stand, Vady went over to the cornettist, a cousin of his, and, borrowing his cornet, sat down on the curb and began to blow. Such sounds! Vady puffed and the cornet wailed! Then to my everlasting embarrassment he snatched off his hat and, with a nod of pity toward me, passed it among the curious spectators.

The collection wasn't a great success. Something like a dollar forty-eight, as I remember it. Those poor old nickels and dimes loomed up, to my eyes, like a monument to sin. When we reached home Vady calmly put them in Iris's piggy bank. You can't win with a man who has absolutely no inhibitions.

"Come on," Vady said, snapping me out of my reveries. "We'll see how good a judge of human nature you are. You pick out the fisherman. I'll ask the questions."

"Don't try any shenanigans, now," I cautioned.

A little farther on I saw my man. He was working with his gurdy and seemed to be having a bad time. He had a mean-looking face, anyway. Secretly I hoped he'd poke Vady in the nose and put an end to games.

As Vady swung himself up on the bow of the boat and walked around to the stern, I moved on down the float, not wanting any part of this experiment.

I was looking for more prospects when Vady caught up with me.

"How did it go, Sherlock?" I asked.

"No go. He let on like he couldn't understand English, but he could talk it. I found that out for sure when he cracked his knuckles on the gurdy. Pick someone who isn't working."

"There," I said, nodding toward an old fisherman who sat on his afterdeck, whittling away on a stick. "That's your man, relaxed, lonesome, and willing."

He was a pudgy little man, gnomelike, with cheeks that hung down in fat little folds. A "snoose-chewer." (No one in Alaska would think of calling snuff anything but snoose.) His lower lip protruded with his cud.

"Don't you go away now," Vady told me under his breath.

"Hello," he hailed the fisherman, stepping onto his boat.

"Why, hello there, pard," said Heavy Jowls, kicking a box toward him. "Come set. I was just makin' me some plugs. These here Arlingtons is a good plug, so's a Olson, but how can a fellow down below know what a fish in Alaska wants? They go to work and paint 'em the all-firedest colors, red and green and yallow"—phew-ee! Out went a squirt of brown cud juice—"and some pink and orange. Now, who in the world ever hearn tell of a pink herrin'? They's herrin' all over the basin today. Looks mighty fine." Phew-w-w. Vady ducked. Heavy Jowls laughed. "Wind's in the wrong direction," he said. "Get any on you? That's a joke I hearn once. Pretty good, eh? Get any on you? But these herrin'—looks good for plenty o' feed this year. Always like to see a good run o' herrin'. I've seen the salmon follow up a good herrin' run. Lots o' times. I use to work on a herrin' boat up around Sitka. Herrin', to my way of thinkin', is the best eatin' fish they is. It's a funny thing now, herrin' wasn't thought much of as an eatin' fish till along about '17. It was right along in there that they got this here Scotch method o' puttin' her up. Since then they can't seem to get enough of 'em."

"You doing any trolling?" Vady put in quickly as Heavy Jowls paused to spit.

"Lord, yes! Trollin' all the time. Just got in yestiday, goin' out tomorrow. You know, pard, it's a damned shame to take a good eatin' fish like a herrin' and use it for fertilizer. Why don't they take some other fish for fertilizer? You take a damned turbot, for instance, what's the good of a damned turbot? Little, bony stinkers. Slivers o' fish, turbots are. O' course a herrin's bony, but not like a damned turbot." Spit. "Oh, I've hearn tell they's some that eats 'em, but I wouldn't eat a turbot if I was starvin' for whiskey. Now they're payin' us trollers five cents a pound for scrap fish, 'tain't wuth cleanin' for that, then they turn right around and make fertilizer out o' tasty fish like a herrin'. Some o' the boys get so riled up about it, they'd burn down the reduction plants, claim it's starvin' out the salmon. I dunno—I just take it easy and I get salmon. Plenty of 'em. When I was—"

"You're just the man—" Vady interrupted, but Heavy Jowls wasn't through yet. Not by any means.

"—seinin' out o' Sitka we had a cook aboard useta put herrin' in pickle. Ever hear of it? No? Well, I don't know what he used exactly. They was onions and—"

"When you bait herring . . ." Vady began, taking advantage of Heavy Jowls's effort to capture that elusive recipe.

"Yeh, onions, and he put spices in 'em, and—le's see now—"

"Do you use a stick in your herring?"

"Sometimes I do, sometimes I don't. All depends. Oh yes," with a satisfied sigh, "a little dash of vinegar. Not much, mind you, 'bout a jiggerful. Some salt o' course. But wait, pard, this'll surprise you—then he fried 'em!"

Heavy Jowls leaned close to peer into Vady's face and note the reaction to his breath-taking announcement. That was Vady's chance.

"Just how do you curve a herring to get that slow roll?"

"It's the bend does it. But them herrin'. They made about as tasty a morsel as I ever slapped a lip over. I'm goin' to fry me up a mess tonight. Sure wish I had that cook's receipt. I could sink my teeth into a mess of them with relish, I sure could."

I'm fond of "herrin'" too, but I was getting mighty tired of them as I shifted from one foot to the other.

"You a fisherman?" Heavy Jowls asked, not waiting for an answer. "Sometimes I think I'll give up trollin' and go back to the seine boats. But why should I? I'm my own boss. Ain't got a worry, own my own boat and catch fish whenever they is any. Just last week brought in eight hundred pounds from Hadley. 'Tain't many, but it's early yet. Most o' the boats is fishin' Hadley this time o' year, musta' bin twenty, thirty. Come in and get me a bottle. Eat good all the time. I ain't no drinkin' man, but I like me a bottle when I come offen a trip. Take a little snifter on my own boat, ain't no harm in that. I don't hang around bars none. Hey, you want a drink?" Heavy Jowls cleaned out his cud with his finger and started to rise.

"No, thanks," Vady said, "my wife's waiting for me. I'll have to be getting along."

"Mighty glad to've made your acquaintance," Heavy Jowls said, sticking out his hand. "I like to meet an interestin' fellow like you. Maybe the wife would like a drink."

"No, no thanks, we really must be getting along," Vady said, backing off the boat.

"There's a man who talked," I said as we made a safe getaway.

"Whew! I'll say he did, and spit, too. Did you ever hear such a verbal barrage in your life? You sure can pick 'em, Babe."

"You learned a lot, too. About herrin'."

"We did learn one thing, anyway. The fleet's at Hadley and ther're fish there."

Of course we went around by the cold-storage dock on the way home. Did we ever miss?

A troller was unloading several hundred pounds of bright spring kings.

"Wait just a minute," Vady said. "I'll ask that fellow some questions.

"Hello," he hailed the fisherman with his usual greeting. "Nice load you have there. Been out long?"

The fisherman looked up in surprise. "We-l-l," he drawled, "not too long."

"Rough weather?"

"Not too rough."

"What were you using? Bait or spoons?"

"Mixed 'em."

"How deep did you have to fish?"

"Varies."

"Many boats there?"

"'Bout the same as usual."

"By the way, where were you fishing?" Vady was beginning to sound desperate.

"We-l-l, I went up to Ernest Sound. There weren't no fish there, so I went somewheres else."

We walked on.

"You sure can pick 'em," I told my crestfallen husband.

I expected he'd want to leave for Hadley at once, but by morning a southeaster was howling. During the week that followed I had an embarrassing experience, made a friend, and learned that other beginners in the fishing game had troubles too.

One evening we had been to a show. On our way home we noticed several people standing in front of the window where I had some pictures on display.

"Let's play a game," Vady said. "We'll go over and look too. Then we'll talk about the pictures. Praise them up, you know. Maybe you'll make a sale."

"Are you crazy?" I asked. "Wouldn't that be fine with my name on every picture! Maybe some of those people know us."

"Nope," Vady said, looking them over, "all strangers. Come on."

He took me in tow and dragged me across the street. Planting himself in front of the window with his feet wide apart, he stroked his chin with his hand. His version of what the up-to-date art critic would look like.

"Beautiful!" he exclaimed, gazing raptly at what I considered a rather poor picture of a boat. His voice would have done credit to the original of Winslow Homer's *Gulf Stream.* "I wonder who the artist is?" He bent closer to the window. "Beth Eberhart. Have you heard of her? Marvelous, isn't it?"

Unobtrusively I tried to get away. He tightened his grip on my arm.

"These must be for sale. We must get one for the study."

The study! I could have killed him!

"Such color!" he raved. "Such perspective. I've never–"

"Good evening, Mrs. Eberhart. Hello, Chief," and there was Chief Monroe standing by my side.

A woman giggled. A man steered his companion carefully around us. Another woman covered her mouth with a red-mittened hand, a mitten several shades lighter than my own face.

The evening had unexpected results.

The next afternoon I had a caller—the lady with the red mittens! As I hung her coat in the closet, I tried to stammer some explanation for the previous evening's disgraceful show. I silently blessed her when she interrupted.

"I know how you must have felt," she said. "My husband is just as bad. But it was funny."

We had established a bond.

Nina Linden was charming. She was slim almost to boyishness, in her slacks and sweater, but there was nothing boyish about her heart-shaped face or shiny braids of heavy blond hair coiled around her head.

She had come out to see my pictures and ask if I'd give her painting lessons. When I told her that we had a troller and would be gone most of the summer, she said they were fishermen also.

Last season had been their first. Just a shade greener than we were when they bought their boat, Clyde had never run anything larger than an outboard motor. Full of enthusiasm and the well-meant advice of friends, they had set out to make their fortune, just as hundreds of cheechakos do every season. They chose Cape Chacon for their first try.

Cape Chacon is well known in Southeastern Alaska as one of the meanest and trickiest of fishing grounds. Located on the southern tip of Prince of Wales Island, its bare, rocky coast line jutts out into Dixon Entrance, fully exposed to the winds sweeping in from the Pacific. Add swirling tide rips that run as swift as a river and you have a picture of Chacon.

Many old-timers avoid Chacon as they would the plague, but not Clyde and Nina. Greenhorns have a special god to watch over them, as we discovered for ourselves. He must have been very busy with the Lindens that summer.

That first day, proving that beginners are often lucky, there was a run of cohos at Chacon. Clyde worked feverishly, taking fish from one line and then another. Nina cheered him on to greater effort. Why, this was better than their wildest dreams!

Some wise informant, either in the spirit of mischief or through his own ignorance, had told them that salmon had to be cleaned at once, not more than half an hour after catching them at the most. Clyde was conscientious. At the end of half an hour he pulled in his lines and, anchoring in a little cove, cleaned his fish. Then they upped anchor and went out for another load. But fish don't wait on the whims of fishermen. The salmon had departed for parts unknown. Although the Lindens trolled until dark, they never had another strike.

That night, through some more mistaken information, they anchored in Stone Rock Bay, an anchorage not recommended by the *Coast Pilot.* During the night a wind blew up from the southeast, driving a huge swell before it. They had tied to another boat for sociability, but now the proximity of the boats was a menace to both. It was too rough to seek other shelter in the dark, so they stood anchor watch all night, doing what they could with anchors and poles to keep the boats from pounding each other to pieces.

In the morning they pulled anchor, heading out into the storm. They reached Ketchikan in the evening, no worse for their experience, but wiser and less trusting. Clyde spent several days in port, repairing the guardrail and a plank broken during that stormy night.

On their second trip they determined to stay in more sheltered waters. Someone had told Clyde that he could catch "scads of fish" with a set line. So, taking his friend's advice, he put out a line. Good luck was with them again. The fish were small, but the main thing was that they were fish, and plentiful. By evening the deck was covered, but it took Clyde so long to clean them they had to wait until morning to sell the load.

"Do you buy fish?" Clyde called out to the buyer as he tied the boat to the cold-storage dock. He was feeling happy and the buyer would too when he saw the load he was going to get. With competition so keen among the buyers he was a lucky fellow to have happened along just then.

"Yes, sir, and yes, ma'm," the buyer called back. "Heave 'em up."

Reaching down into the hold, Clyde pulled out a gunny sack stuffed to the brim. Laying it on deck, he reached in and dragged out another, and another. Grunting with the effort, he threw them up onto the dock.

"Whatcha got there?" the buyer asked, mildly curious.

"My fish," Clyde said, strutting a little in his pride.

"Fish?" The buyer gingerly took hold of the edge of one of the sacks and looked inside. "Good God, man!" he exclaimed. "I thought you had some fish to sell. These things are rock cod. We don't buy them."

Clyde threw the sacks of cod back onto his deck. He lowered himself to the boat, went inside, and put the engine in gear. Carefully he circled the buoy at the end of the reef and headed down the channel on the west side of Pennock Island. With Ketchikan safely hidden behind the island he stopped the motor and hurled his three sacks of rock cod into the stream.

"Between your experiences and ours I guess we've seen about everything bad that can happen to fishermen," I said, little realizing what a naïve remark it was.

Before Nina left we had made plans to do some outdoor sketching together. Of course I knew I'd be going fishing again in spite of my resolution. The Lindens weren't going out until May. I hoped I could talk Vady into waiting until then. It would be such fun to have someone to paint with. We could do a lot in two months.

I knew he wasn't going to like my suggestion, but I hardly expected such strong opposition after his remarks about painting on the boat.

"We can learn so much from each other," I said, "painting together—"

"There's just this much about it, Beth," Vady said, interrupting my carefully prepared speech. "Marriage is something that doesn't stand still. Either we grow apart or we grow closer. If your painting means more to you than I do, by all means paint. You have to make your own choice in these matters, live your own life."

"Do you mean I have to give up painting or you?"

"No, of course not. I can fish alone and you can paint all summer long if you want to, but I can tell you right now that it isn't going to help our marriage. You're not a career woman, you're a homemaker. A hobby is a fine thing for a pastime, but if you let it take on undue importance it becomes a vice, just as everything else that's overdone."

Immediately I tried to put myself in right with him. "I do want to go fishing," I lied glibly. "I only thought it was too early to go out yet, and the boat is so cold in the winter."

"Ever since I came up here," Vady continued, "I've been looking forward to showing you Southeastern Alaska, knowing how much you'd enjoy it. That's why I bought the *Emblem,* so I could take you places. If you don't want to go, I can easily get rid of her."

"I do want to go," I said again, "but since it's been too

stormy to go out, Nina said she'd come over every afternoon this week and we could work together."

"That's quite all right," Vady said, but his tone was cold.

I could feel my cheeks getting hot and the pupils of my eyes dilating as they always do when I get mad.

"Listen here, Vady Eberhart," I said, "let's get this settled once and for all. Don't you like my pictures?"

"It isn't that . . ." Vady said, hesitating for words. "Well, if you want to know—when you're painting, you're so darned exclusive. You don't want my praise or my criticism, it's as if you were living in a different world, shutting me out."

What he said was true, I had to admit. Painting had been a different world, a world of my own creating, and I'd resented any intrusion into it. Then, as the implication of his remarks came to me, I started to laugh. I couldn't help it. He was jealous—of my painting.

"The eternal triangle," I gasped, "he and she and a paintbrush."

My levity didn't help matters any. Misunderstandings of years aren't so easily brushed aside.

"You stay home and keep your appointment with Nina," Vady said. "I was going to call Joe White anyway and suggest we make a trip together. There's bottom gear on the *Emblem* and a good market for red snappers. I can pick up some pointers."

I wasn't very happy about the arrangement and I could see that Vady wasn't either.

"Don't expect me back for a week, maybe two," he said when he left.

"You'll miss me," I teased, trying to relieve the tension between us. "You'll have to do your own cooking, you know." It sounded pretty flat.

I'd miss him, too, I knew, and I hated to have him go with that coolness between us, but my loneliness would be tempered by the enjoyment of having someone to paint with.

It was four o'clock that afternoon when Nina and I put away our brushes after a satisfying day. I looked out the window and there was the *Emblem* easing up to the float. My husband's explanation that there "weren't any fish" didn't ring quite true.

Vady has taught me a lot of things during our marriage. Impulsive by nature, I have learned to avoid snap judgments by evaluating results. All day I had been thinking over our conversation. Just how important was my painting? I knew that for Vady fishing his own boat was a dream come true. Was it fair for me to spoil it for him? Would it finally cause a rift that would never heal in that perfect companionship we had always enjoyed? I knew I'd never have a moment's peace of mind if he went out alone for any length of time, wondering where he was and whether he was safe.

There was only one solution. I'd go fishing this time—this summer only.

Chapter 7

Although the next morning broke dark and threatening, Vady decided we would leave anyway. Those fish at Hadley were like a magnet. "It's only twenty-six miles," he said. "It shouldn't take us over four hours."

"Twenty-six miles are a long way on the water, and nine of them crossing Clarence Strait. A lot can happen on a body of water that size."

"Learn to take things as they come, Babe. Don't always be expecting calamity. You only make yourself unhappy, worrying over something that will likely never happen. Time enough when it does happen. We have to start to make some money from our investment. So far we've been running in the red."

At Guard Islands we turned out into the strait. Gray storm clouds rolled up from the south; the water was dark with a heavy swell making up. When we finally reached the protection of Prince of Wales Island, the wind struck, bringing snow with it.

"Just like old times," I muttered, taking my storm stance, feet wide apart for balance, one hand grasping the window ledge for support. My irony was completely lost on Vady. He picked up his spoons and went out to the cockpit.

What is there about fishing, I wondered, that can change a man's nature so completely? For there was my husband, professed hater of cold weather, muffled to the ears in his sheepskin coat, his fingers as cold and stiff as the herring he was baiting. Yet on his face was an expression of utter contentment.

Seeing me watching him from the door, he shouted, "All right, I'm ready, slow 'er down."

Even at half speed the wind blew us along at a clip so lively the lines wouldn't sink, but stretched out straight behind. It was only by shutting off the motor entirely that we could get them below the surface. Riding the waves, we blew in among the fleet at Hadley.

Now we were really fishermen, fishing with other boats. There must be fish here; these old-timers wouldn't stay unless there were. But how could we detect a strike in such rough water? The poles kept up a continual dance with the motion of the boat.

Hearing Vady call, I stuck my head out the door. "Turn!" he yelled. "You're too close to shore. I have seventy-five fathoms of line out."

Quartering the heavy seas, the *Emblem* rolled so far the tips of the poles almost touched the water. Turning the wheel as hard as I could, I got the bow around quickly to put an end to that terrifying roll.

Vady was yelling to make himself heard above the din of motor and wind. "Straighten her out! Straighten out! You'll run over the lines. You can't make a sharp turn like that. Turn slow. Watch the lines. Keep them straight and taut all the time."

What a dreadful discovery! No matter how much we rolled we had to run slowly! Poor Vady! I'd learned my lesson too late. He reeled in those yards and yards of wire line, patiently untangling knot after knot in the cold, wet leaders.

I've never welcomed dusk as gladly as I did that night! While we went through the narrow opening into the anchorage, Vady stood on the bow and took soundings as we inched slowly forward. He tested the anchor carefully when he let it out, before shutting off the motor.

It was a great surprise to me to see the other boats come charging into the bight full bore, shut off their motors, throw out their anchors, and disappear below deck before the chain had run out and jerked the boat to a stop.

"Isn't that dangerous?" I asked. "Haven't they any regard for their boats? They might easily hit a rock."

"It's not dangerous for them, because they know the anchorage as well as they know Thomas Basin. Most of these fellows have been fishing here for years. I took precautions because the harbor's new to me."

"I'll bet you wouldn't be so careful if you were fishing alone. You'd probably be eating supper by the time the *Emblem* settled down. Speaking of supper, I have a surprise for you. I forgot the meat, it's still at home. I hope you're not hungry."

"The heck I'm not!" Vady said. "Wait a minute. I'll get you some."

If he wanted to make a joke of it, that was fine with me. I was looking through the locker, debating whether to have a can of corned beef that looked like dog food or a can of beef stew and vegetables that tasted like chickenfeed, when he came in with a pan of herring cleaned and scaled.

"If the fish won't eat them, we'll eat them ourselves," he said with a grin.

Heating up the skillet, I cooked up a nice dish of bait for supper, and we enjoyed it very much, thankful as we ate that we hadn't been fishing with worms.

In the morning it was even rougher than the day before, but we followed the boats out. Occasionally we'd see someone pulling a fish. Why couldn't we catch any? We hadn't had a strike. Could it be that the *Emblem* was one of those boats that just wouldn't fish? Some claimed that a Diesel throbbed too much, that the vibration on the lines frightened the fish. Perhaps we'd bought a boat that never would fish.

And we had other problems, for unless we could find where the fish fed we wouldn't catch any. Nor was it that simple. After we located the feeding holes, we still didn't know the answer to the next question. When did they feed? It might be high tide, low tide, or between the tides. Each school of fish seemed to have mess call at a different hour. We must also learn the answers to such questions as: What is the topography of the bottom? How many fathoms of line can we put out with safety? Where are the charted pinnacles or humps? Where are the uncharted pinnacles or humps? Are those patches of kelp growing there, or drifting? Which spoons will the fish take, or would they prefer herring, or plugs? What trolling speed would be most likely to get results?

Having determined the time and place, we were ready for the most important question of all. How far could we run in a given direction without running out of the school?

Each of these little details of fishing lore came to me as a distinct surprise. At the beginning I'd thought we would go out, drop our lines, and catch fish. As we were commercial fishermen, we would naturally catch a great many fish. That was how commercial fishermen made their living.

I didn't know we had to outsmart the fish; as one old fellow put it, "You have to learn to think like a fish."

Did I only imagine the tip of one pole was bent back a fraction more than usual? I called Vady's attention to it, and he reeled it in. There on the very last spoon was a thirty-five-pound salmon, dead as a stick, dragged to death! We hadn't even seen the strike. Half an hour later, for no apparent reason, the line parted at the gurdy, taking to oblivion two heavy leads (worth at least three dollars), forty fathoms of stainless-steel line (about twenty-two dollars), eight rubbernecks, and an equal number of leaders and spoons. Forty-five or fifty dollars' worth of gear, mysteriously lost.

"Let's go in!" I said angrily. "Everyone catches fish but us, and when we do, we don't even know it. We've already lost more gear than we'll ever be able to pay for. I've had enough for one day."

Instead of anchoring when we went into the harbor Vady looped our mooring line loosely around an old piling there. As I watched him I wondered how a rope could slide on its knotty, barnacle-encrusted sides with the changing tides.

The day in the open made the warmth of the galley

seem like a luxury, but it also made it hard to prepare supper and clean up afterward as we relaxed and our eyes grew heavy. Seven o'clock was our usual sack time.

Vady seemed unusually restless that night. "Get over!" I grumbled at last, waking up for the third time to find myself half out of the bunk.

"I don't know what's the matter," Vady said, sitting up. "I can't seem to stay on my own side. We must be listing. I'll have a look."

Before he could get his feet on the floor there came a great commotion outside as the groaning lines finally gave with the weight of the boat and thumped roughly upward on the dolphin. For a moment we rocked violently, then steadied, my distrust of that piling vindicated.

By noon next day Vady was as discouraged as I was. "I can't understand it," he said. "Every time I pull the lines the baits are gone, but we never see a strike. Losing that line has me puzzled, too. A line doesn't break without a reason. I had only forty fathoms out on that line, and seventy-five on the others, so I know we didn't hit bottom. Either those fish are so big our old gear won't hold them, or we can't catch fish. I'm willing to give up if you want to. We could go back to Karta Bay and try bottom fishing. We could still make a trip out of it if we could locate a red-snapper bank."

It was a break I hadn't expected. Two hours later we were in the quieter waters of Karta Bay. After the turmoil of those last two days it seemed like Paradise.

"We should always remember," I told Vady as we rode comfortably at anchor, eating our lunch, "not to take fishing too seriously." I was thinking about what Nina had told me about Chacon and the grounds on the West Coast. Sooner or later, I felt sure, Vady would want to go farther from home.

"I'll be satisfied if we only make expenses the first year," he agreed. "Fellows tell of making six to ten thousand their first year, but it's all hearsay. I've never run into anyone who made that much."

"We can just as well fish close to Ketchikan. No use going to the distant grounds."

Now there was opposition in his voice. Polite but firm.

"Oh, we'll be going to the West Coast about April or May, as soon as the weather settles. There's no use fishing inside waters then. The big loads come from the outside."

"But you said you didn't care about big loads. It's dangerous out there, westerlies every afternoon, nothing but 'blow holes' to anchor in. It's no place for a woman."

"Where did you get all your information?" he asked. "That's ridiculous, Babe. There's just as many safe anchorages as here. When the wind comes up we'll go in. No rough fishing, I promise you that."

That afternoon, as I helped with the ground tackle, I learned to slip half a herring onto a hook without an inward shudder. Then as my husband let out the anchor that held one end of the line, followed by the hundred and fifty fathoms of rope line with its dangling baits, I tried to keep the boat on the course we reasoned must surely lead over good bottom and schools of waiting red snapper. Then he dropped the little red buoy over the side to mark the end of the line.

The sea gulls had caused us no end of bother as we baited up, stealing bait, and even getting away with some herring-baited hooks on leaders we'd made ready for trolling. We joked about attaching tags to the leaders offering a reward to all such gulls that were returned to us. After all, those hooks cost us ten cents apiece.

While we waited for the line to fill with hungry fish

we went exploring. We were surprised to find a boat-building shop in one arm of the bay. It seemed like such a remote location for a business venture. There were several logging outfits and one shingle mill working in the bay also.

We visited the ruins of Old Kasaan, an old Indian village that burned many years ago, where only a row of bleached totem poles marked the site of a once-prosperous community.

We walked through New Kasaan on another arm of the bay, where there was a cannery. It is the home of about fifty Indians who depend for their living on a few months of summer work afforded by the cannery, and on the fishing, hunting, and trapping on their island wilderness.

Twice we circled the buoy, when we went back to pick up our line, before Vady could snag it with the gaff. Shutting off the motor, I went out to watch the fun of pulling it in.

Those were exciting moments as we watched to see what forms of sea life would come up from the depths. Too often it was only an empty hook or a slimy sunburst wound around a bait, but there were also red snappers, brown rock fish, and once a halibut that furnished us with many excellent meals. I'll never know what became of the skate we caught. It was an ugly thing! I merely mentioned that the English were said to be fond of skate wings. Later, when I went out to get it, thinking to have the wings for supper, it had disappeared.

Anchoring in a little bight next day, we went ashore in the skiff to examine a snug little house of weathered, hand-hewn shakes we had seen from the boat. Some hardy pioneer had spent much time and effort in building his home, which now stood deserted. Breakwaters six logs high protected both house and garden from the tides. The root cellar, smokehouse, and woodshed were also built of cedar, silvered to a soft gray by the years. Garden and house were strongly fenced against marauding deer. The whole place showed evidence of painstaking workmanship. There were signs of family life in the flower beds, garden seats, and raspberry canes showing through the snow.

On the opposite side of the bight a less pretentious house was falling into decay. A little powerboat, high and dry on a grid, had great cracks opening along its sides, and the motor was rusting away.

We wondered what had become of the owners and pictured them from the condition of their places. The one, neat, industrious, proud of his ability to wrest a home from the wilderness. The other, slovenly, careless, possibly some old fisherman with no pride in his possessions.

When we returned to the boat, there was a great fluttering aboard. Although we had left our baited hooks on deck, well covered with a gunny sack, a nosy gull had seen a herring, dug it out, and was now tethered to the line. Unable to get rid of the hook or to swallow it, the poor thing was lunging desperately. It was an act of mercy when Vady put an end to it.

The following day we had an encounter with sea lions that nearly scared me out of my wits.

We were trolling in the bay when I heard a "woosh" and saw a broad, flat, hairy head come up a short distance behind the boat.

"Sea lion," Vady said. "Watch this." He tossed out a herring. The sea lion caught it deftly on the surface of the water, dived, and came up blowing a fine spray of water from his nose. He was an immense beast, fully six feet long from his snout to the end of his flippers. He had great big brown eyes, long, drooping mustaches, and wicked-looking yellow teeth with two long fangs that looked ready for whatever might come along.

As he came to the surface again Vady threw another herring. The sea lion caught that one in mid-air. This was fun! Like having our own trained seal. We set the bait bucket on the deck and took turns tossing out herring. Each time the sea lion came closer, dived, and came up showing his ugly teeth in what we hoped was a grin.

At last the bucket was empty. "That's all you get, old fellow," Vady said, but, like the fisherman, the sea lion didn't speak English. He came closer to the boat, raising himself high in the water. We saw his great round body as he dived.

He came up again, his head not two feet from where Vady stood in the cockpit. Vady made a wild leap to the deck. "Go 'way! Git!" he shouted, waving his hat. The sea lion paid no attention.

"I'll get the gun," Vady said. "He might try to get in the boat."

"No, I'll get it!" I cried, heading for the galley. He wasn't going to leave me on deck with that thing leering at me.

"Hurry!" Vady called as I wrenched the gun from its hook.

I ran up on deck. Now there were two sea lions. Our "pet" swimming against the side of the boat, stretching his neck full length, his pal swimming behind.

Vady took the gun and fired once into the air. The sea lions dived.

"Why didn't you shoot at them?" I asked.

"They're protected by law," Vady told me.

A boat, carrying mail and supplies to a newly reopened

mine, passed us as we returned to our anchorage, giving us a friendly blast of greeting from its whistle.

Thinking that we would put out our set line in the morning, and then troll, we had a herring-baiting bee that night, trying to curve them to the exact degree that would give that "sick fish" roll that, we'd heard, never fails to attract salmon. Herring that have been frozen and thawed and then allowed to stand have horrid characteristics. These were definitely not fresh. By bedtime the galley floor, our hands, our faces, even our hair, were plastered with herring scales. From now on, I vowed, baiting would be done outside, regardless of weather.

During the practice session Vady pricked his hand with a hook. Manlike, he refused the Epsom-salts bath I offered to prepare. He woke me in the night to show me his swollen, inflamed palm. It was paining him badly.

We agreed we'd better start for home at once. Fish poisoning is nothing to trifle with. I dreaded the idea of traveling those forty miles at night but was consoled with the thought, gleaned from somewhere, that the water is usually calm during the night.

We were barely on our way when I found how wrong that no-blow-at-night theory was!

I steered my usual zigzag course. How deceiving the shore line was at night. I couldn't tell whether we were miles or only a few yards from the beach.

The moon was at the half and, although obscured by clouds, helped to lighten the sky and show us the driftwood. The words of the *Coast Pilot* kept running through my mind. "During southeast blows, the sea, at the entrance [of Clarence Strait] is rough and treacherous to small craft." The wind was certainly from the southeast!

I was having trouble with the *Emblem*. She seemed determined to take us into danger, hitting the waves at the wrong angle, pulling over toward every piece of driftwood we passed. She bucked and sloughed, turning too far or not far enough whenever I touched the wheel.

"Don't tell me inanimate things don't have personalities," I said. "This boat is like a cantankerous old lady tonight. She's like a waddling, fat old squaw. The Old Lady of Kach Khanna!"

At last we were out in Clarence Strait, straining our eyes for the first glimpse of the beam from the Guard Islands Lighthouse that would guide us across the strait.

I'll never know how rough it was that night, for the spray dashing over the pilothouse obliterated everything but the beam ahead.

The hour-and-a-half crossing seemed like a lifetime. Noticing my nervousness, Vady took the wheel, trying to hold the boat at an angle that would prevent that awful roll that was her habit in rough weather.

Such are the vagaries of Alaska winds that by the time we reached Guard Islands the waves were subsiding. We came into Tongass Narrows in calm water.

When we reached home and Vady was soaking his hand in hot Epsom-salts solution, I found out for the first time how discouraged he was.

"I don't know what we ought to do," he said. "Shall we fish some more or sell before we get in any deeper? We should have loaded up at Hadley. Other boats were catching fish, why didn't we?"

"Don't give up yet." I tried to laugh away his black mood, but my heart sank. He must realize, then, that the whole experiment was a failure.

"We need so much new gear," he went on. "All the lines should be replaced, but we can't afford it now. The stays are just about gone and we should have a new anchor chain. That's the way it goes. It takes money to make money."

"Now, Mr. Riley," I said to myself, "what do you suggest we do about this?"

Chapter 8

The halibut season opens the first of May. Weeks before, the halibut boats began congregating at the fishing ports, coming in from outlying districts. Moorings were crowded as the boats were made ready, provisions were stored away, bait and ice packed into the holds. At midnight on April 30 the race to the banks began.

I'd heard of the halibut fleet, thinking of it as perhaps fifty or seventy-five boats. A steady stream of boats passed our wanigan that night! Too excited to sleep, I stood at the window and watched their lights twinkling from masts and portholes. It was like viewing a marine spectacle. The rhythmic beat of the heavy-duty Diesels sang a sea chanty to the mysteries of the tide, the hidden secrets of the ocean, the beauty of the sunsets, and the courage of the fishermen. Enthralled, I stood there until dawn, when the last of the boats had passed.

The following week was a happy and exciting one. Vady and I had been talking at the breakfast table about the wild animals we had seen on our trips.

"What do you suppose happens when they meet in the woods?" I asked.

"They are probably surprised. Then, unless they are enemies, I presume they each go about their own business."

It seemed a natural conclusion, but I kept thinking about it, and when Vady left for Thomas Basin I determined to paint a picture of an encounter between a bear and a deer. The picture progressed smoothly. I had finished the sketch, a bear rising from behind a fallen log to face a startled deer, when Nina arrived. She was enthusiastic.

"Do you know what you should do, Beth?" she asked. "That would make a good cover for *The Alaska Sportsman.* Why don't you take it down to them?"

I took it to the editor, Emery F. Tobin, with considerable trepidation. To my surprise and delight he bought it! Not only that, he also ordered a picture for a later issue. Vady was as happy over my success as I was.

By the time I had thought of a suitable subject for my next painting it was time to go fishing again.

One robin doesn't make a spring, and since all weather signs had failed us in Alaska, we developed a system of our own for marking the seasons. In the States pussy willows were a sign of spring. With the summer came sunshine and heat. The rains of fall congealed into the snows of winter.

In Ketchikan, where rain is ordinary throughout the

year and temperatures vary but little, we watched the activities of the fishing fleet as our season indicators. When the old-timers began readying their boats for the fishing season it was pussy-willow time down south. Grids were at a premium as boats were hauled out for copper painting. New gear and lines appeared; Tongass Narrows teemed with life as the trollers passed in ever-increasing numbers.

"Now we can fish in comfort," I said cheerfully as we set out for Clover Pass one day in early May.

But it didn't look like spring on the water, for Tongass Narrows was covered with a thin coating of ice. Even though it was broken by the passing boats, it slowed our speed noticeably. Strange that ice would form on salt water when the mercury stood at only a few degrees below freezing. We decided it must be that the fresh water from the numerous creeks along the shore, being lighter than the salt water, lay on the surface and froze.

Perhaps it hadn't been fish poisoning at all, or the Epsom-salts treatment might have cured it. At any rate Vady's hand healed quickly. Now, his good spirits restored, we planned to bottom-fish. We had bought a couple of new skates of gear. If we trolled between sets, the fish wouldn't have a chance.

It soon began to snow. With a bitter wind blowing, and the shore line obscured, by three o'clock we lost all interest in fishing.

Roosevelt Lagoon, in Naha Bay, where there was a Forest Service float, would be a good place to tie up. Rounding Cache Island, we soon made out the ghost town of Loring, which, a thriving community when Ketchikan was born, was now almost deserted. Winding along the narrow channel of the lagoon for a mile, we tied to the float at its head. Three other boats, driven in by the bad weather, soon joined us.

"Do you realize this is the first time since we started fishing that we've tied to a float with other boats?" I asked.

"I hadn't thought about it," Vady said, "but I guess you're right, except that one at Bell Island."

"He wasn't very sociable, remember? At Hadley there wasn't a chance to talk to anyone with the boats anchored so far apart. I like this. It seems more friendly."

The men stood on the float, talking together, and I watched them with envy. What were they talking about? What adventures were they telling? They seemed to be having such a good time! Laughing, talking, slapping one another's backs. Oh, to be a man and be able to walk into their conversation uninvited! But when Vady stepped out on the float all he got were curt nods. The talk died down. One by one the men drifted away and disappeared on their boats.

"Not a very warm reception," I teased. "Do you suppose we'll ever be accepted into the Mystical Order of Fishermen?"

"They are sort of clannish," Vady admitted, "but we'll get acquainted in time. There, what did I tell you?" he whispered as someone hailed us from the deck. "Company already."

"Hello down there!" from the deck.

"Come on down," called Vady.

"Oh no, thanks. Just wondered if you had some onions. Can't eat supper without onions. I eat lots of onions, and every trap-robbin' sucker here's either eaten his or forgot to bring any."

Onions! Phooey! We might as well be hermits, I

thought, as I got out the cards and challenged my husband to a game of double solitaire.

The sight we saw in the morning was well worth the trip. It had snowed all night and now our little harbor was a mermaid's fairyland. Spruce trees bowed their heads under the weight of the snow. The little creek across the way was a thin trickle of gray water between white banks. A deer, foraging for his breakfast, was making heavy going of it. Our boats might well have graced some gay parade, with their white festoons and snow-laden decks.

If only I had my paints! Each window framed a picture of unsurpassed beauty.

Vady, man of all work, hunted for wood for our new stove. Then, although, it spoiled the beauty of the flotilla, he shoveled the snow from the decks. Seizing this chance to do the galley some good, I tore myself away from the window and went below to scrub, hoping this would be the end of those pestiferous little herring scales that had been showing up in unwanted places ever since our baiting experiment.

Before noon the skies lightened. One by one the boats pulled away from the float. We followed them out. At Betton Island we set our skate, then trolled offshore until time to take it in. One of Vady's inventions in the pilothouse enabled me to throw in the power for the gurdy from there. Pull String A to put the gurdy in gear, slip Knot D in string into Notch F in Board B, and so on. A laborsaving gimmick if there ever was one, unless D fouled in F and the whole alphabet went amiss.

When Vady pulled the set line I was busy, trying to keep the boat from drifting over it, but not too busy to step out on deck when he called "Fish on!" to see what briny monster would appear. Usually it was a red snapper.

The tide was causing me a lot of trouble and the *Emblem* was stubborn. No matter how hard I tried I couldn't keep her from crossing the line. Vady was having difficulties too, leading the line from one side of the boat to the other as she wallowed about. Finally he had to stand on the narrow bit of deck abaft the cockpit, hauling the line over the stern.

It was while he was on this precarious perch that he felt a vicious tug on the line. "Fish on!" he called. "A big one!"

I ran out and handed him the gaff, watching breathlessly as the struggle began. It wasn't a fair fight. With only that little bit of deck for Vady to stand on, the fish in its natural element had all the advantage. Some impulse prompted me to root for our side.

"Hold him! Hold him! He's running out! You're gaining on him! Rah, rah for us! Hold him, he's running under the boat! There he is! He's coming our way! Pull!"

Just then Vady slipped! He lost balance and for an agonized minute hung out over the stern. Fortunately for him the fish tightened the line. It was all that saved him from another unpremeditated bath. He made a swipe with the gaff. It missed. He made another, and the fish came over the side, landing in the cockpit—the biggest ling cod I ever saw! Its ugly big mouth gaped open, its eyes popped from their sockets as big as billiard balls. Surely nothing on land or sea needed to be that ugly! They brought only five cents a pound, but their livers were worth a dollar a pound, big livers, too, which made the fish and the liver worth about the same.

"Good fishing!" my husband gloated, gazing proudly at his checker full of red snappers and our last horrid catch. "We'll have time for another set. This time let's try keeping the boat going slowly ahead as we let out the line. That'll stretch it along the bottom better."

I thought it would be an easy matter to keep the *Emblem* on the course, but she pulled over in spite of all I could do. I'll put her in reverse. That'll straighten her out, I reasoned.

One twist of her propeller and it snapped the line in two! So much for my inspiration!

As our new skate sank from sight, I decided that I definitely did not have what it takes to be a fisherman's wife.

That night, when we went into the lagoon, I was more convinced than ever I'd never make a fisherman or even a pilot. Home was the place for me. I made the mistakes; Vady paid for them. Yes, we were partners in everything.

He had told me plenty of times that a boat is not like a car, that I had to steer from the stern while I watched from the bow. But, too cocksure of my ability to make a landing without his help, I swung the wheel hard over to clear the float. A very neat job I thought it was, too, until a crash out back drew my attention. The bilge pump had caught on the float, tearing loose part of the guard-rail!

Vady was very gracious about it, saying anyone could misjudge distance. Perhaps he wouldn't have been so forgiving had he been able to foresee the full consequences of my steering.

Late the next afternoon, when we caught our first salmon since Hadley, some of the damage became apparent, but not the worst. That was to come later in a knockout blow. Now we found that the pump, forced back as it dragged along the float, had hit the gurdy and loosened it. When I turned on the power, there was a terrific clatter as the gurdy rattled against the deck.

"Turn off the power!" Vady yelled. "I can't pull the fish until I tighten the gurdy!"

It seemed to me that we had never had a fish with the vitality of this one! Time and again the tip of the pole bent down as he made one smashing run after another. In his hurry Vady fumbled with the pliers. That fish would get away for sure! While we circled in deep water, watching that dancing pole, I made a vow. Never again would I forget to watch the stern.

At last Vady called to me to turn the power on, and we got our fish, a beautiful thirty-pound salmon. With the lines in and night coming on there was no object in putting the lines out again. The wind had come up, driving a cold rain before it. I was thinking longingly of the comfort of the Naha float when Vady came inside and told me to speed up the motor and go in.

For a few minutes the *Emblem* responded willingly. Then she choked, let out a rasping cough, and stopped!

"Fine place for a breakdown!" Vady said, jumping down the ladder.

It didn't look fine to me! Close aboard the waves pounded on the beach. Spray dashed high against the bare, weather-rounded boulders. How long would it be until we were washed ashore and broken to pieces on those menacing rocks? The *Emblem* had turned sidewise in the trough of the waves and wallowed helplessly.

"Broken coupling on the fuel pump," Vady called. "I can't do a thing out here. We're in a bad spot unless a boat comes along."

Where were the boats? All day they had been trolling beside us, but one by one had picked up their lines and gone in. In the distance there was one little boat. Since early morning he had been trolling, alone, around a rocky point.

If he saw we were in distress he might come to our rescue, but if he went back to the point, we were sunk. With every wave we rolled closer to that boulder-ridden beach.

"Put up a distress signal," I begged.

"It's no use," Vady said. "If he sees the *Emblem* drifting and intends to help us, he'll come anyway. If he doesn't look this way he wouldn't see the signal. We'll just have to wait. If we drift in to the beach we'll have to try to get off in the skiff. I couldn't hold the *Emblem* off the rocks with the pike pole."

We'd never make it in the skiff! That frail, tiny thing would dash on the rocks like a chip! Anxiously as we drifted nearer and nearer to that bedlam of water, spray, and rocks we watched the little fishing boat.

He had seen us! Yes, he was pulling his lines! It seemed forever before he was beside us, ready to take the rope. Vady ran up on the bow. The fisherman, a little Filipino, came as close as he dared in the heavy swell and then came out on deck. Vady coiled our line and gave it a heave. It fell short. He pulled it in and coiled it again. The other boat circled closer. The roar of the surf, close beside us, was deafening. With the boats threatening to bump together, Vady threw the line. The fisherman caught it, secured it quickly to a cleat, and got under way. The backwash was sweeping around the stern of the *Emblem.* "We've cheated you this time," I thought. "But will we always be so lucky?"

The other boats had moved into quieter water and were still fishing. So, being the first ones in, we tied to the far end of the float to leave room for them when they came in. I was getting very touchy about the other boats.

No matter how crowded the float might be, not one had ever tied a line to the *Emblem*. The *Emblem*, her battle-scarred sides fairly shouting, "Welcome," remained totally alone.

Alaskans had the reputation of being hospitable and friendly. Why were they making an exception of us?

While we had our soot-flinging oil stove, I'd placed the blame on that. Our new wood-burner was sootless. Other boats, however, belched black clouds of soot-laden smoke and no one seemed to mind. We were outcasts. Hadn't the onions proved it? How I wanted to belong. To come in to a friendly atmosphere at the end of the day, to exchange the gossip of the fishing grounds, to be hailed by name and accepted as an equal!

Even Vady felt it. Although he laughed at my vehement resentment, he seldom made his friendly advances any more.

After our early supper I moved into the pilothouse to watch the boats come in, while Vady worked below on the fuel pump. Fortunately for us he had a spare part and needed only to put it on.

Several new boats had joined the fleet. The float was sure to be crowded.

I had it! I'd lay a trap!

Seeing a boat entering the lagoon, I rushed outside to line our bumpers along the guardrail in a protective row, then stood on the bow ready to take a line and throw it expertly over our bollard. Surely this would work! With a broad smile of welcome for the poor, tired fisherman, I fancied I looked both expectant and friendly. There was plenty of room for the troller along the *Emblem*'s side.

Now the boat was abreast! Why didn't he come out and throw me a line?

The motor growled in protest as it was thrown into quick reverse. The boat almost turned a back flip. Backing and maneuvering, she finally slid in behind us. Third boat out!

Frustrated, I went below, but half an hour later I was back in the pilothouse for my evening eavesdropping. I'd watch them, yes, and listen to them, too. They couldn't see me in the dark pilothouse unless a beam of light happened to shine in.

Then I saw it! The impossible had happened! Snuggled in beside us, her lines in a friendly embrace across the sturdy bow of the *Emblem,* lay the *Ruth.* In my woe I hadn't even heard her come in.

Satisfied and happy, I settled down for my evening's entertainment, although snatches of conversation were all I ever heard.

"Where'd you catch them minnows?" a fisherman asked, peering into his neighbor's checker.

". . . hell, no, I ain't been to Kasaan. Whaddya take me for, a damned fool?" . . . "Hear Ole went on the rocks. 'Bout time you was goin' aground, ain't it, Spud? You ain't been on the rocks since that time in Snow Pass. God! How I laughed when I seen you high and dry on them rocks. Your old matchbox topplin' there at forty-five degrees. Spud's a gonner this time, I said to myself." One of the men lighted a cigarette and the match flared up. Someone saw me and they moved off down the float. "Got a fifty-pound soaker today, right off . . ."

Well, I could always go to bed, even if it was only seven o'clock. It had been dark for a long time. I had forgotten to bring my pajamas this trip, so in lieu of something better I crawled into a pair of the mate's longhandles and scrambled into the bunk. Then I heard a woman's voice on deck. "Anybody home down there?"

"I'm not dressed," I whispered to Vady. "Go up and—"

Too late! Vady was already gallantly escorting her down the narrow ladder.

Embarrassed but pleased to have a visitor, I asked her to sit down. She was a young woman with a little boy nine months old. He was a vigorous youngster. She couldn't hold him still for a minute.

"We just came today," she said. "We're on the *Ruth.* I just happened to see you when someone lit a match on the float, so I decided to come over. There aren't many women with the fleet this time of year. It's nice to see one."

"I'm glad you came," I said, clutching the sheet self-consciously around my neck. "I enjoy meeting the people from the other boats." Far be it from me to let her know I never had.

"I suppose you're an old-timer," she said. "This is my first year."

"No, this is our first season too." The baby wanted to play. I put out my hand and he grabbed my finger in his fat little fist.

"Isn't it hard to keep him amused all day? He must about wear you out."

"He does. I have to hold him all the time except when he takes a nap. It doesn't give me much time to get things done. He's such a husky, too."

I looked down. The sheet had slipped and there was all that extra yardage of my makeshift pajamas, hanging limply in folds and wrinkles all over my body.

"My husband's making repairs on the motor," I said foolishly, pointing to distract her attention while I yanked at the sheet, hoping she hadn't noticed my resemblance to a loose-skinned Brahma cow.

"Your boat is awfully nice," she said. "It has so much

room. Ours is a lot smaller, real crowded with the three of us, and of course I have to have Jimmy's diapers drying overhead all the time."

She thought our boat was large! This bird cage!

Jimmy wanted to play peekaboo. I played peekaboo with one hand, hanging onto the sheet for dear life with the other. Vady's amused glances didn't help a bit. I was getting more and more embarrassed.

"We lost most of our fish today," my visitor was saying. "That old fellow, Hard-Luck John, says when they strike but won't stay on, they're moving in and haven't started to feed yet. He says they'll be feeding tomorrow and we'll have a good day."

"Perhaps that was why we didn't catch any at Hadley."

There went the sheet again as I reached out toward the baby. Then a thought struck me. What of it? She was a fisherman's wife. By her visit she had accepted us. She didn't care what I wore. Half-worn, long-legged woollies or royal ermine, it made no difference. Now we belonged to that great Brotherhood of the North—the Fishermen! Throwing back the sheet, I played peekaboo and hide-and-seek with the baby. I made him cat's cradles and paper boats. I crawled out of the bunk and made coffee, walking on the ends of the underwear that dangled around my feet. It was a splendid evening.

She'd said that tomorrow would be a good day! But our entry in the diary didn't show anything good.

"Easter," wrote Vady. "It doesn't pay to fish on Sunday."

Determined to follow the other boats and fish where they did, we put out at five o'clock in the dark. But the other boats, elusive as café cockroaches, had already scuttled out of sight. No doubt about it, they were bound for that mythical place, which is anyplace you are not, where the fish bite before you get your lines out, and keep a man on the jump until well after dark.

Well, I thought, if they wanted to play hard-to-find, we'd play with them. Away we went, from channel to inlet, from inlet to bay, into harbors and out of harbors. Not a boat did we see! Yet they'd all turn up in the lagoon again that night. Where did they go during the day?

By dusk I was seething. Was this business of fishing to be a closed book to us forever? Ignored by the fishermen, scorned by the fish, we were as popular as a sea lion in a school of herring.

"I'm heading for the lagoon," I snapped, "and I don't care if we never come out again."

But how restoring of hope is a good night's rest! By morning the disappointments of yesterday were forgotten. Eager as ever for what the day would bring, we put out the lines. Seeing two fishermen very busy pulling fish, I went over beside them. Carefully and deliberately I covered every spot in which I saw them catch a fish. I tried farther out; I tried farther in; we went faster; we went slower. All the time they were pulling fish. We hadn't had a strike. Vady used bait; he used spoons; he put on more lead; he pulled in his lines and took lead off. He put out six fathoms of line; he put out twenty, thirty, forty-five. He pulled his lines and put them out again at six fathoms.

The two other fishermen continued to pull fish. I was fit to be tied!

"Fish! Fish! Fish!" I stormed. "I believe those fellows just do it on purpose to show us up. They have some secret we don't know and never will. The whole business is a fraud!"

"Oh, take it easy," Vady said smoothly. "We'll catch fish all right, just give us time."

His entry in the log that night showed disaster. "Lost salmon and whole damned line."

In justification I added a postscript: "Lost only fifty fathoms of our new line. Two twenty-pound leads. Four new spoons, ditto leaders, ditto rubbers. Is one GOOD strike worth this loss? Yes. After almost two months of NO strikes, I think it is."

Then our luck changed so suddenly it left us breathless. We caught fish for several hours the next morning. The boat smelled marvelous!

Of course it couldn't last, but we didn't care. We only wanted to stand in rapt delight and look in the checker, to make sure we weren't dreaming. With the warm sun on our backs we were getting drowsy. Maybe a snack would wake us up. I went below for apples.

We'd been especially lucky around Cache Island, although it was a hair-raiser, knowing the danger that lurked beneath us. I was never sure I was out far enough, or in far enough, to miss a nine-fathom spot that stuck up like a sore thumb in otherwise deep water. It was important, too, with twenty fathoms of line out. The chart didn't help much. A fraction of an inch on paper, but how much room did that give me on the water? I studied it again. I wasn't going to be caught making another mistake.

Satisfied that I had done my duty, to the fisherman, I sat back munching my apple.

"Power!" yelled Vady, and I went into my routine. Snatch String A out of notch. Pull string tight and slip Knot D into Notch F. I heard the gurdy start. Already indifferent to the landing of a fish, I didn't go to the door.

Then, through the window, I saw a pole bending back

from the strain of a snagged line. "Speed up and head for deep water"—I remembered my lesson. I kicked the throttle ahead for more speed. Deep water would be anywhere, for we were surely on that nine-fathom spot. Hearing a great commotion outside, I stepped to the door to see whether the line was coming free.

All morning Vady had been teasing me, in his exuberance over catching fish. I thought he'd acted very ungrandfatherly, dancing on the deck, swinging on the boom like an ape, taking all sorts of foolish chances. What was he doing now, lying across the cockpit in that grotesque position?

"Stop your foolishness," I said.

Then I saw the blood streaming from a cut on his face, and the gurdy stancheon, lying twisted and broken on deck.

"That does it," I choked. "We're through fishing right now. People getting killed all the time."

All but knocked unconscious by the blow on his head, where the stancheon had hit him when it broke from the strain of the snagged line, Vady tried to stand up. He was half blinded by blood and shock.

Both lines on the starboard side had caught and held. Something had to give way. The stancheon, already weakened by that unfortunate landing at the float, had been the first to go.

He had to take in the lines, but it was a laborious task. Weak and dizzy, he waved me away when I tried to wipe the blood from his face. It was all he could do to get the poles up and secured.

At last, with a makeshift bandage on his head, he lay down on the bunk and we started the longest twenty miles in the world, back to Ketchikan.

I blamed myself for the accident. That stupid landing

at the float, and I hadn't been watching the lines carefully enough. Why must it always be I who was ignorant or careless, and Vady who was hurt?

All the way in I was wondering what we would do when we went back to the States, for, of course, our fishing days were over now. Could we sell the boat and the wanigan?

"Not on your life," Vady said after the doctor had sewed up his head and promised that it would heal without a scar. "After all, Babe, it was my head, not yours. Do you think I'd sell the *Emblem?* We're not through with fishing yet a while. A fellow expects a little grief."

Chapter 9

"When does this living off the land begin to pay?" I asked Vady one day. We had stayed home, waiting for his head to heal. "I've made up a little financial statement, and it looks to me as if we'll be living off the Territory instead."

"Don't be so pessimistic," my husband said, laying down his book.

"You must agree that things haven't gone very well. You might have been killed and we haven't begun to make expenses. The budget book is so lopsided it won't even lie flat in the drawer. How simple life was when we had a steady income. Something a person could depend on. Here, read this."

"'*Emblem,*'" he read, "'three thousand dollars.' Right. But you must realize, Betsy, that the boat is an investment. If we only made the interest on our money the first year, that's all lots of small businesses do. The season hasn't started yet, and think of all the fun we've had."

"H-m-m-m," I said doubtfully, "like cutting your head and knocking out a tooth? At the rate you're going, by the end of the season you'll be nothing but a torso."

"All we need is one good load," Vady said, ignoring my mention of his injuries.

"Yes? But what if we don't get one? Look at this: Two dozen spoons at eight and a half a dozen; sixteen rubbers at nine-fifty a dozen; a hundred and five pounds of lead at twenty-five cents a pound; leader wire, leaders, nylon line, and three stainless-steel lines at something over twenty-seven dollars each. It's terrible. You never told me that gear was so expensive, or that we'd continually have to replace it."

"It's an impressive list," Vady admitted, "but I never thought it was going to be all gravy. There are plenty of fellows who don't make a go of it. That guy who bought the *Roly Boy* last summer, for instance. Paid fifteen hundred for her, fished a month, then came in and sold her for a thousand dollars. How long have we been fishing?"

"Three months. But wait. Here's what we've made."

"This ought to be good," Vady said with a grin. "Did you put down that half a salmon?"

"Be serious. Even your friend Riley had to eat. Here's what we've caught: Fourteen rock cod; sixty-one red snapper; seventeen salmon; five halibut (three eaten); one skate (disappeared), and one sea cucumber."

"You forgot the starfish," Vady said.

"There's this much to our credit," I went on, "fish enough in the locker to last all winter. Our friends and neighbors scared to death we'll offer them more scrap fish, and twenty dollars and sixty-five cents in money, the only entry I can make in black ink."

"Red's more cheerful anyway," my husband laughed, pulling me down on his lap. "Stop worrying. We'll come out all right. That's the advantage of a program like ours. If we can't make it one way, we'll make it another. I was talking to the fellow in the fish market yesterday. He wants clams, says he's paying two-forty a gallon, shucked. How'd you like—"

"Can you shuck a clam?" I interrupted.

"Anyone can shuck a clam. Remember that shale beach where the clams were as big as teacups? We could load the boat on one tide and the tides are just right now. How about it?"

With a stack of gunny sacks on deck and our largest washtub aboard, we left at daylight the next morning.

During the first hour of digging we kept telling each other how easy it was. While Vady turned over the gravel, exposing the clams that lay six inches below the surface, I tried to keep up with him, picking them up and throwing them into the deck bucket. It took only three minutes to fill the bucket and empty it into a sack. This was a snap! Why wasn't the market flooded with clams?

In another hour we began to suspect the answer. My husband was dallying along like a school kid before breakfast. "What's the matter with you?" I asked, then tried to straighten up. Ouch! My back! My shoulders! My arms!

"Don't answer," I said. "I can guess. Let's quit. The tide is almost in anyway."

"Suits me," he said, throwing down the shovel. "Let's walk around a bit and get rid of the kinks."

Pausing on a knoll to admire the view, which would

have been beautiful if I'd been able to straighten up enough to see it, I looked down at the *Emblem* riding quietly at anchor in the bight. Against a background of spruce-covered hills, with the blue sky above and gulls wheeling overhead, she made a lovely picture. But something was wrong! Definitely wrong! The background was moving! No! The boat was moving! With deliberate nonchalance, our boat was gliding out toward the open sea, dragging her anchor with her!

"Look!" I screamed. "The boat!"

Vady's comeback was remarkable. He gave one quick look and sprinted down the beach, hurdled a two-foot rock and landed like a flying base runner on the skiff. What a wonderful headline, I thought. "Old Man Changes to Mountain Goat in Seconds."

The *Emblem* had drifted around the point and was moving at a good clip with the tide. Vady was rowing like a crewman in a championship race. By the time he reached the *Emblem* her anchor had found a new hold on the rocky bottom and she was resting placidly on smooth water. What of it? I'd never trust that anchor again!

The sunset was gorgeous. Our new anchorage, 'way up at the end of the bight, had a muddy bottom, good holding ground, so we took our supper to the beach.

We were continually surprised by the number of little cabins we saw, tucked away in remote harbors or standing lonely and forlorn on tiny islands. Deserted homes of mink and fox farmers, prospectors, and fishermen, hunters, trappers, or miners, and some, no doubt, who had just wanted to be alone. They all bore evidence of Alaska's early growth. Ghost towns and ghost villages, beached boats, some burned and some rotting away, half-buried tent frames, all showing the passing of time and man. No one will ever know their stories, the history, romance, and hardship they hide, as tides, winds, and rains combine to erase them.

There were two beachcombed shacks on the island, showing signs of recent habitation. Over the door of the larger one was a sign, pencilled on a board.

"Keep off this plis!"

Plis. Please? Place? We couldn't decide, but as far as we were concerned, the warning was unnecessary. The stench of drying fish filled the air and we had no desire to investigate further.

Then we saw a party of Indians coming in in three open rowboats. The whole family was there—Grandma and Grandpa, two young couples, a brace of small boys, and a toddler of three or four. One of the young women was white.

They immediately took up housekeeping in the shacks, carrying their blankets inside. Soon a small fire blazed nearby and they hung their pots over it. Wires were strung between convenient spruce trees, and they blossomed with a variety of bright-colored clothing. The Indians seemed very comfortable in a remarkably short time.

After they had eaten, Grandpa and the children came down to the beach. The children were as interested in us as we were in them, watching us with their bright, beady black eyes, alert and inquisitive. But when we spoke to them they hung their heads, wiggled their bare toes in the sand, and giggled.

These were Tlingit (pronounced, "Klink-it") Indians from the village of Saxman, about three miles south of Ketchikan. We had gone there once to see the unique collection of totem poles, one of the best in the world. The most outstanding among them, because it was so incongruous among the others, was the Lincoln Totem. A replica of Abraham Lincoln, complete with top hat, standing atop of it.

Legend has it that when Alaska was still owned by the Russians the Raven Clan of Tlingits was conquered by the Eagle Clan. Later, when the United States purchased the Territory, the Indians went to Fort Tongass and pleaded for freedom from the Eagles. They were told that slavery could not exist in any country owned by the United States and that President Lincoln was responsible for their freedom. In gratitude to Lincoln they erected the fifty-foot totem with him on the top and the Raven crest at the bottom.

The Indians had been sealing, the grandfather told us, but they had been as unsuccessful as we had been at fishing. They were leaving on the long row back to Saxman in the morning.

"On Annette Island, there," the old man said, pointing to the large island a hundred yards across the channel, "is town of Metlakatla. White man not live there. Cooperative town for Indians, founded by Father Duncan many, many year ago. Not our tribe—Tsimpshean."

"What do they do for a living?" Vady asked, pleased with this chance to learn history firsthand.

"Tsimpsheans own cannery, own sawmill, own everything. Own water, too. White man not fish offshore. Indians own water."

Was he warning us that we were in Indian territory and had no right to be here? I hoped he hadn't seen the clams stacked on deck. Indians probably "own clams," too.

"Many year ago," the old fellow continued, "more than sixty, someone tell me, survey boat, name *Hassler*, anchor here charting waters. Named harbor for boat. Me, I never saw boat. Too young, didn't realize life yet."

"What was the reason for these co-operative villages?" Vady asked. "How did they begin?"

"Many year ago," the old man said slowly, gazing off into the past, "there were many Indian villages. All small, maybe two, three families, maybe five. Teachers no like to teach maybe seven, nine. All little villages move together. All little kids go to school now, teachers stay. Good teachers, very smart kids. Good."

"Do the Indians have their own industries? Do they do carving? Make baskets?"

"No. No industries, just sawmills and canneries. Much work in village. White man have charge. Indian he do work. Maybe someday he want new boat, white man write check. Indian get fine new boat and fish. Fishing good, maybe he pay for boat this year, maybe fishing not so good, he pay next year. Maybe fishing no good at all, never pay."

"Quite a gamble," Vady laughed, but the Indian's expression never changed.

"How about you, don't you have a boat?" Vady wanted to know.

"My boy Duncan, he fish my boat now."

"How many children have you?"

The old fellow looked puzzled and scratched his head. "Eleven—or eight, maybe." He wrinkled his brow, then began counting on his fingers. "There's Duncan, Margaret, Gloria, Verle, Louise, Benjamin, and Peter—and George—and there's Robert. That's them, nine. One of my boys, Paul, him orpheum."

"An orphan?" Vady said in surprise. "How did that happen?"

"Mother and father he die. Little kid have no home.

My wife hc say, 'We take him. One more little kid no matter.'"

I left them talking on the beach and, taking the Kodak, walked up to the cabin in the hope of getting some pictures.

The women were in the cabin but, hearing me, the grandma came outside. She wasn't very happy about it when I asked to take her picture. I really couldn't blame her. Would I have been if our positions had been reversed? Although I couldn't understand what she said, her motions indicated that she was giving me the Indian version of "What! In these old rags?" But she let me snap it anyway, aluminum hair curlers and all.

Back on the boat we stood on deck to watch the last glow of evening fade from the sky. Nowhere we've ever been does Mother Nature say good night with such a burst of color as in Alaska. Sometimes she bathes the skies with soft yellow and orange, or, if in a bad mood, she piles up great gray clouds, tinting their edges with red and purple. On summer evenings she flings colors with both hands, recklessly mixing every hue on her pallette so one's eyes fairly hurt with the splendor of it.

A pair of eagles soared above us, swooping down occasionally to light in the treetops. Then we saw the reason. High in the tallest tree was their nest, as untidy a mass of sticks and twigs as one could imagine. Through the glass we made out their young ones, about the size of half-grown turkeys, feather-sprinkled necks stretched to full length, greedy mouths wide open.

Vady rowed out to the mouth of the harbor and put out the set line. By the time he came back, the nosee-ums, gnats, and mosquitoes were so thick we hurried down below, got into bed, and put out the light.

A few moments of darkness, and z-z-z-zing! Buz-z-z-z! Those mosquitoes again!

Refreshed after a long day's sleep in the quiet of the galley, they came out in formation, like a flight of bombers. Brave and determined, they attacked, in droves, singly, and in pairs. We fought back with everything we had, and succeeded in killing a few, but when they sent in a cloud of replacements we were utterly routed. We pulled the sheet over our heads and finally dozed off through lack of oxygen and sheer exhaustion.

In the morning, although we left at daylight, the Indians had already gone.

Outside the harbor we stopped to pick up our bottom gear. I was in the galley when I heard Vady call to get up there, quick! He was hanging onto the line. Just standing there, not doing anything.

"Well? What's all the excitement?" I asked, wondering why he'd called me away from my work for nothing.

"I've got a fish."

"Marvelous. Why don't you pull it in, then?"

"What do you think I'm doing? I'm trying to pull it in. It's like trying to raise the bottom."

"You can't tell me you have a fish so big you can't move it."

"No wisecracks," Vady said, "it's a fish. I felt it jerk." He began to pull in hand over hand, an inch at a time. "Find the gaff. Stand by," he ordered, grunting with every pull.

"Aye, aye, Cap. The gaff's right beside you, crew standing by for bottom."

Then I looked down in the water, and there it was! There what was? I would have sworn it was the skiff, only, as it turned slowly over and over, there was first a flash of white belly, then a blur of black back as it laid back on the line, stubborn as an old cow.

"Good Lord! Look at that halibut! How'm I ever going to get that thing in the boat?" Vady's eyes were like golf balls, and he began to shake with excitement.

He was to the leader now. The halibut was leading up easily, but when Vady reached around for the gaff he began pulling back. Time after time Vady would get him near the boat only to have him take off again. At last we horsed him alongside, grabbed the gaff, and gave the halibut a pile-driver blow on the head. It bounced harmlessly.

The halibut went wild. He churned the water to foam. There was no use trying to hold it; that fish had the power of a locomotive. Down it went, and then Vady had to haul it back again a little at a time.

Brother! The idea of getting that thing in the boat with us sent cold chills down my spine!

Again the fish was up beside the boat. "Get the other gaff," Vady shouted. "When I conk him, hand it to me. You've got to help pull him in."

I stepped over into the checker to get closer to operations, not liking it at all. Now the halibut's head was half out of the water. He was certainly ogling me.

Crack! A good blow. The halibut's eyes rolled.

Smack! The gaff took hold. "Grab on here. Get hold. Pull." Vady ordered, gaffing the fish again with the other gaff.

"All together, now. PULL!"

The fish was half out of the water. We pulled with all our might. It was on the edge of the cockpit, balancing there like a gondola with its head and tail upcurved.

It made a lunge, and Vady leaped. He hurled himself at it, landing on its head. The gaff hit him on the ear. His feet flew out from under him. Down they went into the cockpit, with the halibut on top!

What a melee! Flying arms and legs, tail and fins! Fish chowder!

I looked down into the arena. Vady was trying to regain his feet. The battle raged. Now Vady was on top, riding the fish as if it were a bucking bronco. He smacked it with the gaff. It bucked. He smacked it again. It reared. He beat it some more and at last the thing gave up and lay there quivering.

It took the two of us ten minutes to get that ornery, slippery, hideous thing into the checker, where it belonged. At the end we were so covered with slime we looked as if we'd been dipped in Jell-O.

"They're so doggoned ugly I'm actually ashamed to look at them," Vady said. "Even a fish must be embarrassed to have both its eyes on the same side of its face."

"You don't look so good yourself," I reminded him. "After this, when you're bottom-fishing, put a slip cover on before you pull your fish."

We killed it at intervals all afternoon, hitting it on the head with a piece of lead pipe. Halibut fishermen say it takes only one well-directed blow to knock them out for good, but how were we to know that a halibut's snout is its Achilles' heel? We would think we'd heard the last of it when it would begin lashing its tail again, threatening to knock out the deck boards. Experienced fishermen don't try to get those outsized models into the boat, anyway. They pass a rope through the gill and tow them into port. Unfortunately we didn't know that.

It was four o'clock in the afternoon when we reached home. "We'll just shuck out the clams," Vady said, "then go down to a show."

His plan sounded fine but it didn't work out that way.

After trying for several hours, not too successfully, we decided to wait until morning and have our neighbor, Charley Holland, teach us the short cuts of shucking. We covered our wounds with iodine, bandaged the worst ones, and went to bed.

"There's nothing to it," Charley said. "Just put your knife in here right below the neck. Cut the muscle, turn the clam over and cut the muscle on the other side. She'll open right up. Run your knife around the shell, and out she comes."

It would have been easier if our hands hadn't been so sore from the night before. But we soon got onto the trick and finished by noon.

Our shucked clams brought us sixty-five dollars. It figured out at about seventy-seven cents an hour for each of us, not counting the expenses of the trip. I was thoroughly discouraged and took no pains to hide it. "Not very high interest on a three-thousand-dollar investment," I said, and for once Vady agreed with me.

I was surprised the next day when Charley came over on an errand. He was a retired fisherman living alone in a little house at the end of the boardwalk. Hesitantly he unrolled a paper he had brought, a calendar that had apparently been in use for many years. It was faded and torn, fly-specked and greasy to such an extent one had to look closely to see that it was a picture of an old man and a little boy gazing over the sea at a full-rigged sailing vessel. A print of one of Norman Rockwell's beautiful paintings.

"I had this picture for years, hanging on my boat," Charley said. "It is a good picture but not very clear. Could you paint me anodder from it? The same size?"

Could I? Copy a Norman Rockwell? The picture was

at least sixteen by twenty inches. Quite a test of my ability.

"I'll do the best I can, Charley," I told him.

I delivered it the next week and Charley seemed pleased and satisfied.

I went home and looked out the window and there was Charley coming down the walk with the picture in his hand. I met him at the door.

"You forgot to sign your name on it," he said. "I like to show my friends."

"I can't do that," I told him. "Norman Rockwell painted it. I only copied it. It's his picture, not mine."

"Makes no difference to me," Charley insisted. "I want picture by my neighbor."

"I'm sorry," I apologized, "it just can't be done. It would be like signing my name on someone else's check."

Charley shrugged and turned away. Plainly he thought I was being stubborn. For weeks after he'd go inside whenever he saw me. It wasn't until I'd given him a painting of his own house with my name on it in large letters and we'd bought a skiff from him that he never used any more that we became friends again. We named the skiff *Flat-Bottomed Charley* in his honor.

Chapter 10

"We can't fool around any longer," Vady said. "The trollers have nearly all gone out. Thomas Basin is deserted. We'll never do anything around here. We'll either have to go to the West Coast or up around Wrangell. Which shall it be?"

"Wrangell, by all means," I told him, determined to put off that terrifying trip to the West Coast as long as possible.

Wrangell—historic city of the early days and now the "friendliest city in Alaska," according to its chamber of commerce; seventy-eight miles to the north, according to the chart; roughly thirty miles of it leading through turbulent Clarence Strait before we would reach the protection of Ernest Sound.

Fortunately the day we left was calm. The sun shone and the water was perfect. We anchored that night in Vixon Entrance, going in "on the lead." There are many safe anchorages along Alaska's coast, both charted and uncharted, but often the entrances are narrow and constricted, with outlying dangers. Once inside, the harbor usually opens up into a landlocked shelter well protected from winds. Occasionally a harbor that seems to offer the utmost in the way of protection turns out to be a "blowhole." The winds tear down the canyons, first from one direction, then another; williwaws that, in their fury, seem to blow not only from every point of the compass but straight up and straight down as well.

Some hardy pioneer had planned to make a home here and go into a business venture, for there were the remains of several buildings and the pens of a fox farm, all long since abandoned.

One other boat came into the harbor, a dogfish fisherman, we knew by the gear and liver cans on his deck.

Morning began like any other morning. At sunup we were moving slowly along, dragging our gear. With Vady each new day was a challenge. He was busy from morning till night, making up gear, polishing spoons, working on the motor, or taking a turn at the wheel while I cleaned up the galley. He loved every second of it.

I often wished I could keep as busy. He'd coax me to come out in the cockpit with him, but there was usually a cold wind blowing and, not having the advantage of long woolen underwear and a sheepskin coat to keep me warm, I'd soon sneak back into the warmth of the pilothouse. Seeing the trouble he had learning to operate the old-fashioned dog-clutch gurdies, I had no desire to fish and perhaps maim a hand or arm.

While there were times when I was content on the water, my days were usually spent in nervous dread of some calamity that might overtake us. I was thinking of the long hours ahead, the boredom of eternally waiting for fish that never showed up, the long drags from point to point as we moved along at a duck's cruising speed. Then a bow pole bent back with such a vicious jerk I thought we were surely on the bottom!

"We're on bottom again!" I yelled, and shoved the throttle forward.

"Bottom, hell!" shouted Vady. "It's a fish! A whale! Slow down before you pull it off!"

The gurdy protested as inch by inch the fish was dragged nearer and nearer the boat. All at once it shot to the surface in a spray of white water, danced across the waves on its tail, and sounded again. It ran from one side of the boat to the other, tangling the lines hopelessly.

At last we saw it, its blue-green back glimmering, eyes rolling. A huge king salmon, the most beautiful fish in the world!

"Be careful," I begged, "don't let it get away."

"Where's the gaff? Hand me the gaff!" Vady couldn't have been more excited if that salmon had been the first fish he'd ever seen, much less landed.

"Right under your hand. Get him quick before he breaks the leader."

Leading the fish carefully toward the boat, Vady reached out and conked him with all his might. The fish quivered as he pulled it over the side.

I ran for the scales. Forty-six and three-quarters pounds. What a fish!

Fishermen disagree as to what constitutes a "soaker."

Some say twenty pounds; others maintain that it must weigh over thirty. We had no worry on that score. Without a doubt we had caught our first soaker.

We had given up the idea of using bait on this trip and had changed to spoons. It made for pleasanter fishing, for herring are bad traveling companions even when kept on ice in the hold. The ice melted and seeped into the bilge, and while we were using them, we ate, slept, and lived in an atmosphere that reeked with the odor of overripe herring.

Back in the States we had always used the old standbys for our sport fishing—the Millers, Superiors, and McMahons—and we had a good supply of these. We also had spoons that were strange to us: the Cloverleaf, Canadian Wonder, PTH, and the ever-useful Egg Wobbler, a must for cohos and a great temptation to kings, ling cod, and even halibut. Vady had also fallen for the ads of a new gadget, the "clear plastic spoon with minnow lamination. Fish go for it. So do fishermen."

Trolling along, close to the rocks, we were surprised when we had another strike, only a short time after we had landed our soaker. Fishing hadn't ever been like this before! All morning they bit with gratifying regularity, fish that weighed from twelve to twenty pounds. Vady was hilarious and our record was perfect, for we landed every fish.

"We'll never equal that again," Vady said, "never lost one."

"Nor any gear, either, and fishing in strange water. Our luck has changed at last."

My husband always claims I am superstitious. Perhaps I am. Anyway, I wished I hadn't said so much about our luck. It would have been better if I'd waited until we were safely home.

In the afternoon, when the fish quit biting on the ebb tide, we set our skate. Just for fun when we anchored, I put a hand line over the side. It was hardly on the bottom when I caught a twenty-pound halibut. It took a little longer on the second try, but the second halibut weighed forty pounds.

"We're in 'em, Betsy," Vady exclaimed happily, "right over a halibut bank. Our skate will be loaded."

But when we pulled our skate two hours later, there wasn't a fish, and half our baits were intact. Don't count your fish until you have them in the checker. Fish have been, are, and always will be unpredictable.

Before leaving home we'd bought a book on the wild flowers and plants of Alaska. If we were to live off the land we'd supplement our diet with native plants when our supply of fresh vegetables ran out. There were quite a number of edible plants, if we could identify them: wild rice, with its bulb composed of many ricelike grains, a plant used in place of potatoes by the Indians in the early days; wild asparagus and celery; goose tongue, the fronds of young ferns and young nettles, which, we were told, cooked up into tasty greens.

When we went in for the night we went ashore and picked goose tongue for our supper salad. The long, slender leaves were thick and succulent, with a rather peppy flavor. We agreed that we could do with it or without it. We'd still prefer lettuce when we could get it.

"We've fished three months for this day," Vady said, busily icing down fish. "I told you, Babe, it would be like this. Do you feel better about the budget now? A few more days like this one and we'll be right on top."

"Twenty salmon! I can hardly believe it, and such beauties! Only two small ones in the lot."

Right then I was in a mood to think everything was perfect.

For four days we fished close by, returning at night to anchor beside the ruins of a burned cannery where a noisy waterfall lulled us to sleep. When trolling was slow we set our skate with varying results. One day we caught twenty-five dogfish in a spot that seemed sure fire for halibut. Another time we set our skate where we'd caught halibut after halibut, trolling. We brought it up with one of Heavy Jowls's "skinny little turbot" and a wide-winged skate.

But the salmon! That was fishing as it should be! We had fished for an hour one morning without a strike, so Vady went below to shave. He had been gone only a few minutes when we had a strike. He came on a run, without his shirt, his face lathered with shaving cream. For two hours he was too busy to finish his toilet, while the lather dried on his face and the sun burned down on his bare back. Even with a bad sunburn he made no complaint about the delay.

He laughed when I gloated over our catch, but who wouldn't be proud to see a checker full of kings? "One to three hundred pounds of fish a day might be slow fishing to some," I told him, "but not in the company I've been keeping."

The shores were steep-to, the rocky cliffs plunging straight down into the water. We fished so close our poles practically dragged through the trees. Our favorite haunt was the point of a small island that Vady dubbed Point Lizzie, as it had no name on the chart. Approaching it from the south, I'd hug the point. With the lines safely past it we'd make a slow circle and come back, as close as I dared. I'd look up and my stomach would do a flip-flop. "This time," I'd think, "we're surely in for trouble.

I'm far too near the rocks." I'd give the wheel a quick turn and head out for deep water. Nearly always, at that sudden change of direction, we'd catch another fish.

The water was alive with feed, needlefish and eulachons. It's such waters that make men fish-happy.

Although there were from five to ten boats fishing close by, no one had bothered us at Point Lizzie. It was one time I was glad to be ignored. Then on the third day a boat moved in and began our circle, complicating things no end. I often had to swing out to avoid him on the point, after I'd spent half an hour or so on the slow drag around to reach our favorite spot. It was maddening, for it meant another half hour lost to get into position for that quick turn-out and the fish we'd come to expect.

"That should be our fish," I'd say as he passed the point where he'd squeezed us out and landed a fish.

"You can't stake a claim on the water," Vady told me reasonably. "You mustn't take the attitude of the old-timers, that it is all yours because you were fishing here first. He may have been fishing here for years, and resent our being here."

"Just the same I don't like it." And I'd turn the boat and try to beat him back to the point.

On the fifth day, just when we'd decided to stay and load up, the fish suddenly quit.

After we had anchored up, Vady put the skiff into the water and rowed over to another boat that had come in. He came back with interesting news. Someone had shot and wounded a bear onshore that morning.

"Come on, bring the jug. We'll get some nice cool spring water and take a look at those old shacks," he said.

He seemed surprised when we hit the beach that I was reluctant about getting out and wasn't ready to enter into the evening's explorations with gusto. I pointed out that I had no desire to meet a wounded bear in any tumble-down shack, and besides, after three months of examining the ruins of mink and fox farms, trappers', miners', and homesteaders' cabins, outhouses, water sources, beached boats, and sundry other wrecks and discards, I didn't feel I'd miss much if I just stayed in the skiff while he got the nice, cold spring water.

Next day, as we were trolling up Blake Channel, I had a minor victory that I thought proved me able to locate the fish. Vady, the fisherman, was ready to pull the lines and run on, but, seeing a tide rip ahead, I asked him to wait. If I were a fish, I argued, I'd certainly be waiting for my dinner there where those rips met. Sure enough. We had barely dragged our lines into the rip when we had a strike. Vady contended that such a coincidence didn't prove a thing, and in all fairness I must admit he can't always be wrong.

The scenery changed as we went toward Wrangell. The mountains were lower and the timber more scattered, many of the hilltops showing bare and brown. Often there were grassy meadows along the shore, something we'd never seen around Ketchikan. Spring freshets filled every canyon and ravine. We could follow the entire course of a creek, from mountaintop to salt chuck, by its series of waterfalls.

The channel, which had been bright blue, began to take on a greenish cast, then yellow, and finally, where the sun hit, such a dazzling mustard yellow it was hard to believe it was water. It gave us a queer sensation, as if we were plowing through a sea of mud. The mighty Stikine River, with its silt-laden waters, had colored it for many miles. The silt covers the water to a depth of three or four feet, and the salmon lie just beneath it, but it was still too early in the year for the shallow fishing and all we caught were ugly little gray cod.

Wrangell was a picturesque sight as we came into the harbor. Offshore the gill-netters' boats lay at anchor, with their dories strung out behind them. At night the gill-netters put out their nets, and the salmon, swimming toward the river and their ultimate spawning grounds, became entangled in them.

The hills formed a semicircle of bright green behind the town, sprawling along the waterfront in colorful confusion. There were houses of every shade—ocher, red, green, brown, and slate, with several of a bright and vivid blue. Everywhere was the startling golden yellow of dandelions, like patches of brilliant sunshine. To the north the blue-gray Stikine Mountains, their snow-capped peaks glistening in the setting sun, formed a mighty backdrop for this typical Alaskan fishing village.

It was pleasant to tie to the float in the harbor behind a protecting breakwater, to know we would have nothing to worry about that night. We changed our clothes to go uptown.

A fisherman fell in beside us as we walked along the wharf.

"Hello there," Vady hailed him.

"Hi, fellow."

"See you just got in from a trip."

"Yep. Came in from Quiet Harbor. Feelin' pretty good, too. Got a three-hundred-dollar jag, first good haul this year."

"My name's Al," said Vady, sticking out his hand. "Glad to meet you, and congratulations. We haven't had too much so far, but we've done better this trip."

"Long-John Jorgenson," said the fisherman, returning the handclasp. "Been fishing around here?"

By the time we had reached the one paved street of the town, Vady knew Long-John's age, how long he'd been married, the names and ages of his three children, and the location of Quiet Harbor, and had a good lead on the spoons to use there and the depths to fish. He'd also learned much of the past, present, and future of the city of Wrangell.

"You're wasting your talents, my friend," I told him. "The place for you is Scotland Yard. How do you do it? But, look! Did you ever see such dandelions?"

"What do you mean, wasting my talents? I thought I did quite well."

"How do you have the nerve to ask so many questions? I should think after all the time the fishermen have been snubbing you, you'd be rather averse to questioning them. See there! Those dandelions are all of eighteen inches tall!"

Oh, it was wonderful to have my feet on ground once more, and such luxuriant growth. What if they were only weeds? I hadn't seen anything like them since we had left the States. With the smell of spring in the air, the bursting cottonwood buds bringing a nostalgic memory of my childhood home on Lake Chelan, and the sight of rich black loam, moist and cool, for the planting of seeds, I had a longing for a garden, to dig in the soil once more, to plant seeds and watch them grow! If only fishing left time for gardening too.

"Long-John was glad to answer my questions," Vady said, breaking into my thoughts. "Everyone likes to talk about himself. Wouldn't you be happy to tell it if we had a big load?"

"Such size! Such color!" I marveled. "Did you notice the dandelions?"

"Say, what's the matter with you, anyway?" Vady

asked pithily, coming to a halt and looking at me closely. "Haven't you ever seen dandelions before? You act sort of balmy."

"What made you tell that fellow your name was Al?" I asked when we got back to the boat.

"I always do," Vady said, "but I never can make it stick. Someone always comes along and yells 'Vady' at me and the deal's off. Valdimure Albert. Now, isn't that a fine name for a fisherman!"

In the morning we made the acquaintance of "Bollard Bill," a fisherman who shared his wealth of knowledge without any cajoling on our part. He told us of a couple of lagoons where, if we were lucky, we could run our boat over the rapids at high tide and find wonderful fishing. None of our experiences so far led us to believe we were that lucky. We'd leave those fish for Bollard Bill. For an hour he entertained us with fish stories, even going so far as to mark his favorite haunts on our chart. The friendliness of Wrangell had not been overestimated. Even the fishermen talked.

We decided to sell our fish, ice up, and go to Quiet Harbor, hoping to duplicate Long-John's catch. The cold storage was so crowded with boats it was afternoon when we finally got unloaded. What a thrill when we received our fish slip! One hundred twenty-five dollars.

"Wonderful!" I enthused. "A hundred and twenty-five dollars for five days' fishing."

"It's not so much," Vady said. "We should do that in one day, but it helps. If we can do as well or better on the way home it won't be too bad."

As it was then too late to go on to Quiet Harbor we ran over to Woronkofski Island and fished the afternoon out around Elephant's Nose.

We watched with amusement an Indian fisherman who

towed his wife behind in a skiff all afternoon. Or could it have been his mother-in-law? There she sat, stolid in her wrappings of blankets, a fish pole sticking out over the side of the skiff. If she made a move, we failed to see it, and the wind was icy. Were they having a quarrel, and was this his way of having the last word?

Chapter 11

We reached Quiet Harbor the next afternoon, eight hours and four fish from Wrangell. Now, I thought, we'll be settled for a few days, and what a spot! At the head of the bay a little creek wound its way between grassy banks. In the evening I'd take the skiff and search that green meadow for wild flowers. The waters of the bay were well protected. It looked delightful.

One round, and Vady hailed a passing troller. "Hi, there, any good?"

"No," came the answer. "I only caught one all morning. I'm going in and anchor up until the tide changes."

"No use staying here," old Wanderlust announced to my dismay. At this very moment our discouraging informant was pulling a fish! We had talked of little else but getting to Quiet Harbor since meeting Long-John. We were here, the anchorage was perfect, the surroundings beautiful, and now he wanted to move on without giving the fish a try!

"That beats me!" I said hotly. "You know Long-John loaded up here, and now you want to move on. All you want to do is run, run, run! What is this, a fishing trip or a sight-seeing tour?" I was beginning to sputter in my indignation.

"You heard the fellow say it was no good."

"Yes, and you saw him pull a fish ten seconds later. Is there any reason—" But Vady had disappeared into the galley. I heard him flop down on the bunk, and, peeking down, I saw that he had picked up a book.

"Where do you want to go?" I shouted.

"I don't give a damn where you go."

Very well, old man, I thought, I'm not giving up Quiet Harbor so easily. Swear and sulk if you like; I'll show you there are fish here. You'll be darned glad to come up and pull them.

I went over water that looked good enough to eat (for a fish). I used the technique of frequent outward turns. Shamelessly I followed that fish-catching boat so closely I was afraid at every turn I'd find our lines tangled together, and I kept it up although I often caught him looking at me in a very unpleasant way. Nothing brought results. Then I hit bottom! That brought Vady from below on the double.

Now it was my turn to sulk. Going below, though it was real punishment for me to ride down there, I spent a miserable hour on the bunk.

When I came up we were out in Clarence Strait, headed into the most unpromising stretch of water I ever laid eyes on. Everywhere were pinnacles—nasty, rocky fingers pointing to the sky, small islands and large islands with forbidding rocky shores, patches of growing kelp hiding heaven knows what dangers. Every menace to navigation in the book. We studied the water through glasses, got out the charts and laid courses, flipped the pages of the *Coast Pilot* and studied the compass.

At last we gave up. Even if we passed those barriers safely, fishing would doubtless result in lost gear, perhaps worse. We'd go in somewhere for the night and then go back to Ernest Sound in the morning.

All day the sun had been bright, making a glare on the calm water. Now our tired eyes began playing tricks on us. Far down Clarence Strait, where common sense told us there was nothing but open water with a range of snow-capped mountains behind it, we saw what looked for all the world like an immense iceberg floating in mid-channel. Even the glasses failed to dispel the illusion. Lemesurier Point, jutting far out into the water, seemed to be an island floating in the air. Union Bay was a river, running first uphill, then down. I felt like Alice in Wonderland in a world suddenly gone topsy-turvy.

"We can put into McHenry Anchorage for the night," Vady said, still cool toward me. "There's a moorage dolphin there."

"McHenry Inlet," I said firmly. I had been reading the *Coast Pilot* too, and knew the inlet was closer. Then, because I was still miffed about the Quiet Harbor deal but determined to be polite, I added with forced sweetness, "All right, McHenry Anchorage, if you'd rather."

But Vady wasn't going to be outdone in politeness either. "The inlet will be fine, Beth, if you'd rather go there."

Both places had disadvantages in the form of hidden

rocks and reefs. As we neared the entrance to the inlet I couldn't distinguish between an island and the peninsula, for the sun was still casting strange shadows. It just wasn't my day, so rather than take a chance on hitting a hidden rock that showed on the chart, I gave up and headed for the anchorage.

Clarence Strait had resumed its normal appearance now that the sun was lower. Our iceberg had melted, showing itself to be merely the reflection of the mountain peaks in the water.

As we went in we saw the bulbs of the giant kelp to our right, growing from the rocks the *Coast Pilot* had mentioned. This is the kelp with the long, hollow whips that reach down as much as sixty feet sometimes, to anchor to the bottom. The hollow bulbs, with their green-brown ribbonlike leaves, float on the surface. It is seldom safe to disregard the warning of a kelp bed, although there were a few times when we anchored in one at night when there was no harbor available. These kelp beds had been proved by other fishermen to be free from dangers, and the kelp calmed the ground swell to some extent. Usually, though, there are rocks just under the water that bare at low tide.

From the Fishery Products Laboratory in Ketchikan we learned to make pickles from the whips of this kelp. Cut in half-inch slices, they were attractive circles with a hole in the center. The pickling process and a judicious amount of food coloring turned the unattractive brown into a bright and appetizing green. The flavor retained a suggestion of iodine.

At the head of the anchorage one small troller rode at anchor. Onshore were the usual decaying buildings, of a mink farm long since abandoned.

We later learned that the onetime owner had been

quite a character. He had done a great deal of work on his place, even to a large boat shed where he had built his own boat. He'd had a fine garden and had once told a friend in Ketchikan, "There's everything out there—rutabagas, spinach, parsnips, carrots, anything you want. Go out any time and if I'm not home just help yourself. Be sorta' careful when you walk around, though. I've got a dozen and a half wolf traps set in the garden and around the house." In other words, "Go out and play hide-and-seek with my ground mines!"

The *Coast Pilot* had recommended McHenry Anchorage as being protected from all winds except a westerly. It was a west wind that blew in that night, making our berth an uneasy one.

With an early start we hoped to reach Ernest Sound in time for a good day's fishing. We were anxious to get back to see whether the fish had shown up again.

The *Emblem* had showed signs of a cold the day before. She'd sneezed and sniffled and made a good deal of fuss about it. But she didn't complain when we started up, so we thought she'd thrown it off.

The waves still wore their white nightcaps as we pulled anchor and got under way. For some reason the entrance looked entirely strange, not at all as it had when we came in the evening before.

"Come and take us out of here," I called to Vady. "I'm afraid. The channel is so narrow and I don't know where the rocks are."

"There's nothing to it," Vady said, taking the wheel. "What are you afraid of? It's four hundred yards or more across. How can you miss?"

Just then the *Emblem* had a coughing spell and the motor stopped.

"What now!" Vady grumbled. He pressed the starter button. There was a sickly whirr.

"Keep trying the starter," he told me as he went below. "What the heck—"

Now that we had lost headway we turned sidewise and were drifting toward the rocky point on the other side of the entrance. Jagged rocks showed through the kelp heads at the surface of the water. I pushed hard on the starter time and time again. The motor wouldn't start!

"We're drifting on the rocks," I shouted.

"Keep pushing that starter!" Vady yelled, bounding up the ladder. "I'll drop the anchor."

The anchor chain rattled over the side. Too late! There was a rasping jar! The grinding of metal against rock as the keel struck.

Vady ran for the pike pole. Thrusting it against a rock, he pushed with all his might. He couldn't move the boat! The tide was going out! We were stuck!

It was appalling. One moment the *Emblem* had been a thing with life, flexible to the turn of the wheel, continually in motion. Now she was dead! Rigid, except for the tremors that went through her when the waves dashed against her side.

Almost imperceptibly she began to list. "Gather up the things we'll need," Vady said, hurriedly untying the skiff and getting it over the side. "Hurry! I'll take you ashore."

What would we need? My mind was in a turmoil. The binoculars there on the sill. I snatched them up. The Kodak. I grabbed it from its nail on the wall.

"I'm ready," I said, and scrambled into the skiff, taking the center thwart to leave room for Vady. Carefully he lowered himself into the bow as I mechanically picked up the oars and started to row. The skiff, tiny and cranky, rocked perilously! There was a scant six inches of freeboard. Water poured in through the seams. Seams that had opened up from the warm winds of the last few days.

"Row! Row harder!" Vady said, his voice rasping.

"I am. I can't."

"We'll never make it. The waves are coming over the side."

This was a nightmare. It couldn't be happening to us. Then Vady made a miraculous move, something he never could have done under ordinary circumstances. Without turning us over he shifted to the seat beside me and took an oar.

"Row! Row! Row!" he chanted. "Pull when I do. Pull harder!"

I was pulling as hard as I could. I still didn't fully realize our danger.

"When we get a little closer I'll just step out," he said.

A quick glance at the water. No bottom in sight! He'd just step out, and walk on the water? Who did he think he was?

Our legs were soaked when at last we hit the beach. Vady jumped out. "Come on, get out," he said. "I'll go back and do what I can." Quickly he pulled the skiff out and dumped the water.

"No, don't go back," I begged. A quarter of a mile offshore the *Emblem* had laid over on her side and was taking a terrible beating as the waves pounded against her.

"I've got to," Vady said. "She'll never last until the tide turns. We'll need food, bedding. Go to the head of the bay and ask that troller for help. There's a Coast Guard station at Lincoln Rock—ten miles—tell him to go."

He was already in the skiff.

How could I leave now? What might happen to Vady while I was gone? Waves of fright seemed to roll over me, leaving me limp. Vady motioned for me to go, and I turned and stumbled up the hill.

Outward signs of religion never have been a part of our lives. What we have within we keep to ourselves. I don't believe God cares what position our bodies are in when we ask Him for help. He has answered as many of my prayers when my hands were in dishwater as He has when I was on my knees. I believe He hears us and cares for us whether our prayers follow a given pattern or are uttered in half-formed, stumbling words. He has never failed me.

"'Our Father Who art in–'" I panted as I fought the stubborn brush that clung to my feet and ankles. "Please, God, take care of Vady," I begged as I waded through a muskeg bog. Would I ever get there? Driftwood cluttered the beach. I crawled over a boulder and under a slippery log. At the head of the bay was a steep, rocky bluff that went straight down into the water. I mustn't fail now, I couldn't. I *had* to get help.

There at last was the little boat, riding as calmly at anchor as if there were no danger in the world. I screamed as loudly as I could. "Help! We need help!"

There was no answer from the boat. No sign of life.

Some way I'd have to get closer. On hands and knees, holding onto every place that offered a handhold, I crept along.

I yelled again and again. At last a reluctant head appeared in the doorway.

"We're wrecked!" I called. "On a rock! Will you go for help?"

"You'll be all right," the head said indifferently.

"You don't understand," I called. "We're wrecked! Stuck! Can't get off! Need help. Will you go to Lincoln Rock for the Coast Guard?"

"Can't," he said, "I'm vorking on my motor." And to my horror he started back into the cabin.

"Wait!" I cried. "Can't you understand? The boat is high on a rock. Breaking up!"

"You're in a hellova fix," he said, and disappeared below.

I'd have to go back and tell Vady I'd failed! What would I find when I got there? I was shaking with anger, shock, and disappointment as I turned back.

I heard a motor. There was the little boat putting out. He had been joking, then. Perverted humorist. But he had gone for help! I could forgive him anything.

The trip back seemed to take hours. At last I could see out over the water. The *Emblem* was lying over on her side. I could see into the hold, vertical now, where Vady was shoveling out ice, battling to save the boat.

On the beach were the things he had brought from the boat. Nothing had been overlooked. There were food and dishes, silverware and cooking utensils, charts, ship's papers, and the *Coast Pilot*. There was our book on Alaskan wild flowers, and the July 1943 issue of *The Alaska Sportsman,* which we always carried for its article on edible wild plants. That, with the fly rod, the .22, and the .30-06, would help in case we ran short of food. He had brought along a deck of cards for entertainment. Blankets, pillows, and sheets were piled on top. There was the jar with the change we'd had when we left Wrangell. The hundred-dollar bill we'd received Vady had put in his wallet and buttoned securely into his back pocket. He had covered the pile of supplies with the tarp, which could be fashioned into a shelter if we were marooned for days or even weeks. We wouldn't suffer for anything.

What a failure I had been in a crisis! Me, with the Kodak and binoculars!

I'd have to move our supplies to higher ground before the tide turned.

And when the tide turned, what would happen then? If the rocks had pounded a hole in the *Emblem,* would she fill with water and sink as she was, lying on her side?

There was the little boat! But what was he doing? Standing well away from the *Emblem,* he came out on deck, stood there for a long moment, watching, then turned and went back into the pilothouse. He was going back into the harbor, not going to Lincoln Rock after all!

When I went for help I'd found we were on a small island that had once been cleared. On the high ground above the beach was a small shelter the size of a pup tent. I carried our supplies up the hill and piled them in the shelter.

Then I hurried back to the beach. The tide had turned! The beach was covered with water.

"God," I prayed, "we need Your help now as never before."

A tiny white line appeared along the deck. The boat was lifting with the incoming tide!

Little by little, as the tide crept in, the line broadened. The poles straightened and at last our boat was standing motionless on the rock.

Vady crawled slowly out of the cockpit, his wet shirt clinging to him, saw me on the beach and waved, then raised the anchor. Taking the pike pole, he shoved the boat out into open water. She floated!

He disappeared inside, and then, I couldn't believe it! The *Emblem* turned under her own power and went slowly into the harbor.

Vady was safe! Nothing else mattered. My prayers had been heard and answered. Now that the dreadful anxiety was over, I was weak and dizzy, my knees gave out, and I sank to the ground. Sometime later Vady found me in the shelter, asleep. I never knew how I got there.

He seemed undisturbed. "Come on, get up," he said, "we've got work to do. You can't sleep all day. We have to move all this stuff back to the boat before dark. It's going to take longer than it did to move it off. Not so much incentive," he laughed.

"Are you all right?" I asked, clinging to him. "Is the boat safe?"

"We saved her! I sure didn't think we would. Lord, we were lucky! What a battle! Getting that weight out of the hold was what did it, gave her a chance to rise. Why didn't you get help like I told you? He was coming out again as I went in, but he turned and followed me back. What's the matter with that guy?"

"He's a savage!" I said. "He refused to go for help."

"It takes all kinds. I was never so surprised in my life as I was when that motor started. Strangest thing I ever saw. It stopped again when I got inside and wouldn't start. Must be the water just leaked inside the batteries then. Come on, Babe, pick up a load."

How could he be so calm after such an ordeal? We might have been having a picnic on the beach for all the signs he showed of what he had been through. Didn't he have a nerve in his body? I was still trembling and weak, with cold chills racing one another up and down my spine.

We loaded the skiff and rowed back to the boat. My husband made a quick checkup. Fortunately the *Emblem* wasn't leaking badly. The hand pump would take care of it easily. With two anchors out we were in no danger of drifting. For the time being we were safe. No telling how long we would be here, as we'd just have to wait until a boat happened by. Vady rowed over again to the troller, but he was back in a few minutes.

"What did he say?" I asked anxiously.

"Nothing. That is, nothing that will do us any good. He's the orneriest cuss I ever saw. He said something to the effect that it wasn't his hard luck and he couldn't watch out for all the fishermen that wrecked their boats on the grounds, and then he as good as told me to get the hell out of there. There wasn't anything the matter with his motor; he just came out to take a look. He's sure a funny-looking fellow—must be a wino or a hophead."

"Darned white of him," I said sarcastically, "to put himself out like that. I hope we run into him again. We'll scuttle his boat."

We suddenly realized we hadn't eaten all day. Half an hour later we were having our dinner, one reconditioned, bilge-water-soaked salmon that had hidden itself in the hold. With most of our things still on the beach, we cut the fish up with Vady's jackknife, fried it without fat, ate it with our fingers, and agreed it was the best meal of the trip.

About five o'clock we saw a boat coming into the harbor. We took turns with the glasses trying to make out the name on the side, wondering whether he would come to our rescue.

"She's the *Cora* from Ketchikan!" Vady said at last. "I know that guy. He'll help us out. I know he will."

Vady rowed over while they were dropping the anchor on the *Cora*. He came back smiling. The *Cora* was on a halibut trip. The skipper had promised to leave at daylight for Lincoln Rock. But he did even better for us. At dusk we saw him pull anchor and head out.

On the fishing grounds, as elsewhere, it takes all sorts of people to make up this queer world of ours. Apparently the god of the cheechakos had not deserted us. We had been through one of those grueling experiences I had read about, yet we were unharmed and safe on our boat. I couldn't convince myself that we had been particularly lucky, as Vady insisted. I was only thankful we hadn't lost the boat or our lives.

Shipwreck was no excuse for idleness, Vady thought. Early the next morning I was astonished to see him take the paint can and begin painting the deck. There was plenty of cleaning to do below, with the oil from the bilge covering everything. As I cleaned, I wondered about the future. Would Vady be willing now to give up fishing? And if he weren't, what other disasters would overtake us before the season was over? I longed for home and our former quiet life, when I went on the water only when I wanted to, and when conditions were perfect.

At three in the afternoon we saw a gray Coast Guard boat come into the harbor. She crept in slowly, a Coast Guardsman standing on the bow taking soundings. They weren't taking any chances of going aground.

Two members of the crew turned out to be old buddies of Vady's. Although I couldn't see where the humor came in, they seemed to think it was a hilarious joke to find him stranded.

At four we were in tow and under way. Vady stayed with his ship as all good captains do, but as I had already shown myself a deserter I chose the larger and steadier *Northern Light* for the long ride home. We breathed a sigh of relief when we had passed the rocks in the entrance.

I've never been so near to being seasick as I was watching the *Emblem* on the end of the towline, sheering first this way, then that, riding high on a wave, then slipping into the trough. The boys were doing nothing to ease my mind.

"Look at 'er now," one would say. "I saw her rudder that time."

"The chief's having a rough ride," another would add. "Hope he makes it all right."

The youngest member of the crew, a mere boy, always added a heartfelt "Whew!"

When it was too dark to see more than the outline of the *Emblem,* the boys came inside with their reports. "I can still see the boat, but there isn't a sign of life aboard." How consoling!

My sympathy and worry for Vady were all for nothing. When we were within five miles of Ketchikan they brought the *Emblem* alongside, and Vady came aboard. He looked surprised when the boys asked him how he liked the ride. "Fine," he said. "She rode like a duck. Why?"

Why, indeed!

Why that intricate system of wires the boys were using to keep the pots and pans on the stove as they prepared supper? Why did the coffeepot slide off the stove, in spite of the wires, and land with a crash on the deck? Why? Maybe my skin is always tinged with green.

Rough or not, the Coast Guard boys were pleasant hosts. After a supper of fried ham, fried potatoes with onions, and baked beans they kept me entertained until we reached home. We played two-hand cribbage for ten miles, four-hand from Meyers Chuck to Caamano Light, gin rummy to Guard Islands, and two-hand cribbage again to Ward's Cove, where we picked up Vady. I could have won a fortune that night if we had been playing for stakes, which merely goes to show that no one is unlucky all the time.

At one-thirty the next morning we tied in Thomas Basin. We had come fifty-two miles during the night.

It was several days before we could get the *Emblem* into the marine ways. Vady came home with the report.

"We need a false keel, new stem, some planks on the bottom, and a plate for the rudder. The motor and generator have to be completely overhauled. The starter needs fixing and the wiring will all have to be gone over. I'm having all the batteries recharged now, and of course she'll have to be repainted inside and out. We were lucky, as usual, Babe," he finished, absent-mindedly rubbing the scar on his head where the stancheon had hit him the month before.

"How long must this go on before you're willing to give up and admit we're beaten?"

"I can't understand your attitude," Vady said. "If our house burned down, would you give up and say we had to live in a tent the rest of our lives? We didn't lose the boat. There's nothing that can't be repaired. We have the whole season before us."

"This is going to cost us an awful lot of money. There surely are easier and less dangerous ways to make a living."

"We have an investment there," Vady pointed out. "Would you rather just let the boat go than have it fixed up, with the chance of making it back this summer?"

"No," I said wearily, "I suppose not. That's the trouble. You always have the best argument. I wish I could one time be right."

"It's easy," Vady said with a smile. "All you have to do is think like an adult."

Chapter 12

While the *Emblem* was on the ways we saw a lot of the Lindens. Clyde had quit his job at the hardware store to get his own boat, the *Skookum,* ready for fishing. When Vady wasn't busy on the *Emblem,* he'd go down to the basin to help Clyde, or if Clyde wasn't busy he'd go out to the Northern Machine Works and do what he could to help Vady.

Clyde was short and well built, with a winning manner and the most devilish eyes I ever saw. He and Vady were a lot alike, both good-natured and full of fun, and either would rather tease his wife than eat—although heaven knows there was nothing wrong with their appetites.

When the men were going to be busy all day, Nina

and I often took our paints and sketch pads and caught the bus to Clover Pass, or maybe south to Mountain Point. We'd take a lunch and spend all day, and as we worked we learned a lot about each other.

One thing I learned very shortly was that we weren't going to be as compatible with our painting as I'd hoped. One day we sketched two tugboats beside an interesting group of barnacle-encrusted pilings. Later Nina asked me over to see her finished painting.

It turned out to be two huge orange circles surrounded by red and black squiggles that covered the canvas. I made the horrible mistake of saying, "What is it?"

"Our sketch," Nina said, giving me one of her wide-eyed glances. "Don't you remember the tugboats? Of course it's the mood that counts and I think I caught it rather well, don't you? I'm calling it *And Seagulls Mieuwing*. Clyde said I should have named it *Borsch at Midnight*. He doesn't have the least appreciation of art, but I wish he wouldn't say such odd things."

There wasn't much I could say except that I didn't understand modern painting. We didn't discuss it further.

When she played the piano for me that afternoon, I found her to be an accomplished musician. She was equally proficient with the violin. She showed me her wood carvings, which were beautiful. Her original designs were realistic and exquisite renderings of native flowers and plants. She was talented and clever in many ways—some of them rather unusual, I thought, when she described the layettes she had made for three pet monkeys they had once owned.

Nina, small and youthful for her years, was one of those personalities you like a lot or not at all. I liked her. She was free from the stuffier inhibitions, a bit of a madcap, but a gentle dreamer, too. She took life casually, or, rather, she took what suited her of reality and filled in from some flexible world of her own. You got occasional glimpses into this dream structure of hers from the startlingly irrelevant remarks she sometimes made in what you'd thought was a logical, serious conversation. On first exposure she seemed like a scatterbrain, too frivolous for some tastes, but men—and women who liked her—felt protective toward her, as if they should shield her from the realities that eluded her.

Before they came to Alaska, Clyde and Nina had lived in northern Idaho. One day they decided to see the world, so they simply sold their belongings and with little more than the clothes on their backs hitchhiked to eastern Washington. There they worked in the fruit harvest for a couple of months, then went on to the coast and took a freighter to Alaska. To me it all sounded very daring and romantic for a man and woman in their late thirties.

"After Alaska, what then?" I asked.

"Oh, I don't know. Maybe farther north. We like it here, though, so we'll likely end up being sourdoughs." Which, in Alaska, is equivalent to old-timers.

"I dread next month," I told her one day.

"Why?" she asked, her eyes wide with surprise.

"I just don't like it, being on the boat. It's so small and cramped. And I don't like the water. I know it's silly and I try not to show it, but I'm afraid of the water. We'll be on the boat all the time, with no chance to get home between trips."

"If you don't like it, why do you go?"

"To be with Vady, of course. I'd rather be with him and be afraid than be at home and afraid anyway, worrying about him because he's on the water."

"It rains," said Nina, which was no news to me. Then

after a brief retreat into thoughts of her own, "I love it. But of course I'm not the homemaker type like you, and I don't much care how I look."

"You can't keep clean on a boat," I said. "That's one of the things I don't like about it."

"Most can't, but you can. I'll bet a horse you can."

"No one can. You'll see. I'll never understand it. I spent the first twenty years of my life on Lake Chelan, where we always had skiffs and enjoyed them, even had to row to school. Now I'm nervous as a gravid seal every minute we're on the water. But there's Vady, born and brought up in South Dakota where they didn't have water enough to wash their ears, and he's crazy about boats and hasn't the slightest fear of the water!"

"Maybe Vady likes to wash his ears."

While I was trying to fit that possibility into the foregoing conversation, Nina remarked, "I'll have it cut."

"Have what cut?"

"My hair."

"Oh no! Not that long, lovely hair!"

"It's dangerous. Twice I've heard of women getting their hair caught in the gurdy and almost getting scalped. One was a little girl."

Yes, Clyde and Nina would be good fishing partners, refreshing together or apart.

One month to the day after we'd been towed in, I went with Vady to see the *Emblem* slide down the ways where she had undergone her renovation. Although she had been insured, the usual deductions of the insurance company had left us with half the repair bill to pay ourselves. Our bank account was as flat as Vady's morning pancakes.

"She's better than a new boat," he beamed, eying her with pride. "Everything about her is just like I wanted it. Motor, fishing gear, wiring and stove all in perfect order.

Fresh paint inside and out and new planks in her bottom. I'll bet she won't leak a drop. It was worth all we went through to know our troubles are over."

"Knock wood," I told him. "I hope you're right, but a thousand dollars seems like a high price to pay for such doubtful assurance."

The *Emblem,* resting on the water as lightly as a lily pad, her white sides shining and gray decks gleaming, her poles straight and tall with their white tips clear-cut against the blue of the sky, certainly made a picture to delight the heart of any fisherman. Inside the pilot-house had been transformed with pale green paint and the galley walls were as purely white as a hospital operating room. There was pale gray on the table, bunk frame, and even the tiny sink pump. Squatting at the end of the galley, the big old Diesel looked like a fat green toad, a newly painted toad all ready to hop.

"I only wish we could afford a new motor," Vady said. "It's poor economy to try to keep an old one running. Besides, I don't know a thing about a Diesel."

"You fixed it that time in Clover Pass."

"We were lucky, just happened to have a spare part."

"Get some more spare parts, then."

"Good grief, woman," he laughed, "we can't carry a complete set of parts. Do you realize what you're saying? That would mean a complete engine, knocked down. Otherwise how would I know what we'd need? Don't worry, I have the more important things, ordinary things that might go wrong. The old boat can't fool Daddy. Nothing's going to happen. We're all set for the West Coast now."

At the dread words "West Coast" the butterflies jumped to life in my stomach. They always did at mention of a trip, only this must surely be a plague of locusts. Butterflies are more gentle creatures.

I tried to derive what comfort I could from the fact that Nina and Clyde would be with us. A partner boat could be a great help in time of trouble. Vady had said I mustn't worry, and certainly we were better equipped than ever before, even to a trim two-passenger skiff in place of the cranky affair that had nearly been our undoing.

Now that a definite time had been set for our departure —that is, weather permitting, which is always the deciding factor in Alaska—Nina and I spent many hours working on our lists of what we should take for our season on the grounds. Clyde and Vady were taking care of the provisions and gear, Nina and I the clothing, personal necessities, and linens.

"Shucks," Nina said after we'd discussed and rediscussed, added to and subtracted from our list, "why worry about all that? I'll take a couple of shirts and two pairs of jeans for each of us. When the legs get dirty we'll cut them off."

With our recent shipwreck in mind I, the practical, thought it a good idea to know what we could use for food, and how we could use it, in case of disaster, so Nina obligingly went with me to the Fish and Wildlife Service's Fishery Products Laboratory. There we found a dainty red-haired home economist in immaculate white, up to her elbows in a pile of slimy sea cucumbers. Those flabby, warty, greenish-brown monstrosities looked like anything but food, yet Redhead explained that the Chinese and Filipinos have been eating them from the beginning, or shortly after.

She showed us how to cut off the heads, split the watery viscera, and retrieve the five long, slender sections of white muscle. These, she said, could be boiled, fried, ground for chowder, canned, frozen, and their flavor was like that of clams but even more delicate and delicious. She served us potato chips with freshly made sea-cucumber dip that proved her point—to me. Nina politely refused the dip, and I must admit I would have found it even tastier if I hadn't seen the essential ingredient first.

Some of the sea-cucumber skins were being sent to the States to be tested as a possible source of leather. How far will scientists go, looking for an experiment! Redhead showed us octopus tentacles, skinned and cut into bite-sized pieces and looking very appetizing in glass jars, and gave us hints on the preparation of sea lion, porpoise, muscles, barnacles, and a few other seldom-suspected sources of food from the sea. It was all very interesting, but I left the laboratory hoping that if shipwreck were to be our lot, we'd be marooned somewhere we could look to the land for emergency rations.

We left two days later, early in the morning, just as the first faint glow of dawn began to brighten the mountain-tops. By our early start we managed to cheat ourselves out of two hours of good sleep, for almost immediately we ran into fog.

Steering by compass course, we headed for Warburton Island, where there was a beacon light. Watching anxiously for the buoys that marked the channel, we moved cautiously in, then shut off our motors, tied the boats together, and drifted while we waited for the fog to lift. Whenever we lost sight of the light we'd start up and creep in again until we located it.

By ten o'clock it had cleared somewhat and we started out.

The two-hour crossing of Clarence Strait was punctuated by frequent fog banks. After running blind for fifteen minutes to half an hour we'd burst out into bright sunshine again.

Cape Chacon was all Nina had said, the shore line bare and ugly, with rocky cliffs and wind-swept trees. Offshore a wave bared a rock in a foam of white water.

Two miles beyond, sheer bluffs rose straight from the water's edge—a rugged coast, wind-beaten and desolate, with numerous rocks and breakers close in and a string of breakers farther out to sea—an awesome sight.

"We're lucky," Vady said. "Such a grand day to come around the cape."

"Grand!" I echoed. "What's grand about it?" Nervous as a witch, I wiped my sweating palms on my slacks.

"Everything. Sun shining. No wind. What more could you want?"

"Calm water," I said, taking a firmer hold on the wheel.

The ground swells, rolling in from the ocean, were getting larger by the minute. The tide rips were making up.

"There's no wind," Vady repeated. "I love these swells. Just like a roller coaster. Fun."

"You can have 'em, and roller coasters too. We're going into the fog again, the worst bank yet. Yellow and thick-looking."

Ahead of us a yellowish-gray fog bank stretched from beach to horizon. Soon wisps of mist floated by the window and the sky darkened and was shrouded by the mist. We were in a world of cold and dismal twilight, gray and depressing. There was nothing left in sight but the *Skookum,* a dim and wraithlike troller following in our wake.

Vady set our course well out in the channel to avoid the dangers near shore. The combination of lazy ocean swells, swirling tide rips, and masses of floating kelp with embedded driftwood made navigation a nerve-racking business.

There was no way of knowing how far we had come, for we often had to slow down to work our way through the drift. I wanted to scream. Instead I stood by the open window, hands clamped to the wheel, dank hair blowing against my cheeks, taking orders from the navigator on the bow.

"Better slow down," Vady warned. "I don't know where we are, but I think I hear breakers."

Just in time! Dead ahead were the great gray forms of the rocks onshore, with the surf pounding at their feet!

I jerked the throttle into reverse! Looking back to see that the *Skookum* was in the clear, I saw a smooth green wave. It rose, curled under; with a hiss it ran smoothly, then broke in a spray of white water. A rock, jagged and cruel, leaped from the foam not two boat lengths away!

The worst part of this whole business, I thought, was that I seemed to be the only one who ever got excited or scared, no matter what happened. As we backed out, away from the rocks, Vady came in from the bow.

"What are you shaking about?" he asked with a grin, giving me a poke in the ribs.

"That breaker! Didn't you see it?"

"Of course. We didn't hit it, did we?"

There it was. We didn't hit it, so what did that make me? Nothing but a coward.

The *Skookum* came alongside. "The fog seems to be getting worse. We'd better go back. Nichols Bay, this side of Chacon, is a good harbor. We'll try to make it before dusk," Vady yelled, and Clyde agreed.

So back we went, not knowing, of course, whether we were out far enough from shore to miss the rocks, or perhaps too far out and in line with the breakers along the reef. Then the skies began to lighten and the sun burst through. Wonder of navigators! There lay the bay, bathed in sunshine.

After a day of anxiety I would have been glad to spend the summer, yes, the rest of my life, in this secluded cove. But the next morning was clear. We left at daybreak.

At last we were on the West Coast, where Dall Island, most southerly of the Alexander Archipelago, was bathed on the outside by the waters of the Pacific; where Cape Muzon, its southern extremity, cheerfully called the "graveyard of the Pacific," overlooked the waters of Dixon Entrance. Going into Cordova Bay, I could see that Vady had been right. Everywhere were the numerous small islands we had been accustomed to, the bold headlands, the harbors and inlets, and the hills were as plushily green as at home in Ketchikan.

My husband, all enthusiasm now that we were really here, was up at three-thirty in the morning rarin' to go. During those longest days of summer the dusk of evening melts into the dawn of morning so quickly there seems to be no night. Was this the same man who yawned so sleepily over his eight-o'clock breakfasts at home? No sooner were we in the bunk, it seemed, than he was climbing out to start the fire, while I stood around rubbing my eyes, trying to get back into the still-warm clothes I had just taken off.

Now fishing was serious, our vacation over. If the *Emblem* meant to pay for her rejuvenation, now was her chance. No more leisurely trips to shore in the skiff, no more runs to places of interest just to see the sights. The cohos were in, and Vady was all business.

On the third day of fishing we realized we were in something of a spot. Here we were with several hundred pounds of fish and no place to sell them short of Ketchikan or one of the buying scows farther north. Early cohos soften quickly, even when iced, and we didn't want to lose our fish.

Clyde, thinking the grass might be greener farther north, suggested the scows. Nina was all for going back to Ketchikan to pick up some things she had forgotten. Vady was neutral, so that left Clyde and me in the majority. Even Tlevik Narrows couldn't be so bad as Chacon, I argued, although we'd heard some hair-raising tales about Tlevik, too. Only the winter before, two men had lost their boat when it hit the turn buoy in the narrows and split wide open. Many small boats had had narrow escapes when the force of the current had hit them broadside, threatening to capsize them. It was well known that during high tides and big runouts the turn buoys towed completely under. Of course, like everywhere else in Alaska, there were rocks in the channel to be avoided.

While Vady spent the evening poring over tide tables and charts, I sat beside him torturing myself by picturing all the mishaps that could overtake us in those raging waters.

We were on our way by four the next morning to catch the high slack tide in Tlevik Narrows. As we approached them the water ran swift as a river. Following the shore line, Vady took advantage of an eddy, and we moved along steadily. I was waiting for the really bad water to come, and bracing myself for the ordeal, when he pointed up the channel to the Waterfall cannery. Thanks to his calculations we'd hit it at just the right stage of the tide. We were through the narrows!

We went ashore at Waterfall to see what is known as the model cannery in Alaska. Although it was not yet in operation, we walked through the clean, well-equipped cannery buildings and saw the rows of neat cabins provided for the hundreds of workers, some of whom come up from the States each year for the short canning season. When we went back to the boat, we gave a halibut to one of the cooks on a tender where we were tied. Before we left he came over with two big sirloin steaks, two pounds of butter, a loaf of homemade bread, and a dozen doughnuts, still warm. It was the best trade we ever made. Owing to a shipping strike, a far too common occurrence in Alaska, supplies had been low in Ketchikan. We hadn't had meat or butter in two months. Now we felt like kings. We invited Clyde and Nina over for supper, happy that we could give them a real treat.

At Port San Antonio we saw our first fish scow. It was built on a log float with the receiving room in the center, the store at one end, and the icehouse at the other. In a second story on one end of the building were rooms for the buyer and his wife and a helper.

The buyer weighed in our fish, then, as we watched, packed them in crushed ice, carefully filling the cavity of belly and head, arranged them in large boxes, covered them with more ice, and stacked the boxes in the fishhouse. Within a day or two the packer would come out from town, bringing ice and supplies for the scow, load on the fish, and take them to Ketchikan to be shipped south.

Seeing the work involved, the careful handling of the fish, I began to realize for the first time the tremendous scope of the fishing industry. I had never thought of all the steps necessary in getting the fish from water to market. Now the rise in price on the way from fisherman to consumer seemed more justifiable. That day we received seventeen and a half cents a pound for our large red kings, but later in the season the price went to forty cents a pound. The packer carried them for two cents a pound. The buyer in town and the several processes there each take a toll of a few cents—all this before the fish are loaded on the ships for markets in the States.

As the boats came in we went out to watch them unload. It was a disgruntled lot of fishermen who sold at San Antonio that night. The weather had been rough and uncomfortable for fishing. The best boats had seldom brought in more than twenty dollars a day. When they learned that we, the greenhorns, had sold a hundred-seventy-five-dollar load, we became the center of interest. Several boats decided to go back to Cordova Bay with us the next day.

Twenty dollars a day may sound like money, but many factors bring down the average earnings of the season. Weather, the most unpredictable of all, is also the most costly. A high wind often keeps the boats harbor-bound for days and results in hundreds of dollars' worth of lost time. Fog, common during the summer months, is particularly bad on the outside banks. Only a hardy fisherman well acquainted with the waters will venture out into fog. Anyone who has had experience with motors knows even the best of them are subject to trouble, and a broken part can hold a man up for weeks while arrangements are being made for replacements from town. Worse yet, a breakdown might result in a long, expensive towing job to the nearest machine shop. Broken poles and gear result in many lost hours during a season that is short at best.

Although we had left Ketchikan with the intention of returning in a few weeks, I felt that Fate had intervened when we learned there would be a buying boat in Cordova Bay.

"That settles it," I told Vady. "We'll fish Cordova Bay all summer. No more Chacon until fall, and believe me, my boy, that's soon enough."

Chapter 13

Entering a strange harbor for the first time is never without a thrill. Returning from San Antonio, we crossed Kaigani Strait just as the blue shadows of evening were darkening the hills. The sinking sun made a dazzling path across the water, making it hard to find the opening we were looking for.

"The chart shows a clear entrance except for a rock that bares at half tide, and some p.d.'s on the right," Vady said.

"What in heck are p.d.'s?" I slowed the *Emblem* to half speed. Whatever they were, I wasn't going charging into them without knowing.

"Rocks. Position doubtful."

"Great! Rocks so well hidden no one knows where they are. I'll shut off the motor and drift in."

"Don't be foolish," he said. "You're past them all already. A tugboat could come in here safely. Just keep to the middle of the channel."

The little bight at the head of the bay was crowded with trollers. Two fish traps, later put out at Cape Muzon, were anchored at the mouth of the bight. The boats either tied to them or anchored close by. The *Bluebird*, buying fish for a Prince Rupert concern and selling supplies to the fishermen, made the little cove as convenient as a small village.

Kaigani Harbor, one of the safest in the Cordova Bay area, is a beautiful place. The entrance, about a mile long, leads to a half-moon bight at its head where boats lay, well protected from storms, behind a rocky point. The surrounding hills are low, with forests of spruce, hemlock, and cedar rising from the water's edge.

We counted twenty-four boats as we came in, nine of them seine boats from Hydaburg, an Indian village farther north. Although essentially built for seining, these boats are used the year round, for both pleasure and profit. An Indian without a boat in Southeastern Alaska is a lost Indian indeed. By changing their gear with the seasons they fish from early spring until late fall, with tables and chutes for halibut, poles and gurdies for salmon, and, later, turntables and rollers to handle their nets while seining. During seining season the larger boats carry crews of from four to eight men.

The seine boats, limited to a length of fifty feet, are beamy, making the trollers seem small by comparison. A flying bridge where, during seining season, a lookout stands to watch for schooling fish, stands atop the pilothouse. There's a wheel in the little watchtower and even on the trolling grounds the Indians prefer to steer from above.

Being a gregarious race, they usually have company on their boats, friends, sons, or other relatives who go along for the fun. Trolling is taken lightly, as they depend upon seining as their main source of livelihood.

Most seiners carry large skiffs equipped with heavy-duty outboard motors. The favorite evening pastime when in harbor is to launch a skiff, attach the motor, and spend the daylight hours making tight circles around the harbor and boats at full speed, the main idea seeming to be how close a turn can be made without tipping the boat over. At Kaigani the roar of the motors, which lasted until dark, sounded like a prolonged Fourth-of-July celebration.

Seining lasts until early November. Then gear is stored for the winter, but the boats are never idle. There is still the trapping season, when they are used as a base camp in preference to a cabin on the beach. The Indians like to travel, often making trips on their boats to Ketchikan, Craig, Klawock, and south to Massett, British Columbia, to visit friends and relatives.

Once during the summer two seine boats on their way to Massett were stormbound in Kaigani. Although equipped only for a crew of eight, each boat carried twenty people. It was too much for Vady's curiosity. He had to go aboard to see how it was done. Babies in arms, toddlers, children, grownups, grandmas, and grandpas swarmed over the boats, all ages, sizes, and shapes. The galley stoves belched smoke from morning until night as the women busily cooked meals that lapped over into the next. One old fellow complained that he hadn't had breakfast, although it was then two in the afternoon. He thought he was due for the next handout, as the kids had all eaten.

Of course there was no place to sit. The space was all taken up by sleeping babies, rolls of bedding, and stacks of provisions. At night blankets were laid out to make improvised beds in the hold.

I tried to picture a group of white people under the same conditions, crowded, tired, and cross. Not so with the Indians. They were as happy and good-natured as a bunch of Boy Scouts at a circus.

"I should think you'd have a good many disagreements, crowded in so close together," Vady said. "It must be pretty uncomfortable."

"We're all brothers," one of the older men told him. "We have the same grandmother. I agree with my brother. My brother agrees with me."

As a result of this happy party the *Bluebird* had to make an unscheduled run for supplies. The first foray of the Indians cleaned out the supply of pop, candy, gum, Kool-Aid, fruit juices, oranges, and canned fruits. Soon all catsup, meat sauces, apples, pastry, and boxed cookies were gone, as the Indians bought out the supplies in the order of their importance to them. Then they exhausted the supply of rice, potatoes, bacon, fresh meat, macaroni, and flour.

Many times during the summer I stood by while one of the Indians did his evening shopping, and marveled at the patience of Gladys, the storekeeper. When fishing was good and money plentiful, they usually spent the days' profits, buying one or two articles at a time and asking Gladys to add up the amount after each purchase. Finally, when the shopping was finished and the Indian had gone back to his boat, Gladys would breathe a sigh and turn to the next shopper, glad to know she had one customer waited on and out of the way. In a few minutes she might look up to see the same Indian back again, all ready to start over, one purchase at a time.

We soon became acquainted with the fishermen on the other boats, as we congregated in the evenings on the deck of the *Bluebird* or stood on the trap logs watching the boats unload. It added a lot to the interest of fishing. It was always exciting to see who would bring in the largest load. It was especially gratifying when it was the *Emblem,* as sometimes happened.

Even a congenial couple like Vady and me were glad of some diversion when we came in at night after being confined all day in quarters no larger than a country outhouse. The enforced proximity was trying enough for married people, but far more so for two men fishing a small boat together, with nothing more in common than the desire for a good season. They were inclined to become grumpy and often tempers flared to white heat over something as trivial as too much soda in the morning hot cakes. Feuds developed and they either split up or fished the season out itching to get at each other's throats.

On the surface Gideon Jones and Frank Doolittle were doing as well as could be expected of men with such opposite natures. Frank, whom we took to be a white man, was known as "Old Soot" among the other fishermen for obvious reasons. He was about forty, by his own admission "hard of seeing and hard of hearing," and he had a befuddled brain. Gid was a young Haida Indian, well educated and likable. Old Soot's boat, the *Dare Devil,* must have been named in her heyday, when she was far more rakish than we knew her. She was painted a sort of muddled color, one half the deck dirty orange, the other half red, the hull several shades of gray with dashes of black tar where seams had opened up. The blue boom was usually draped with salmon halves drying in the sun.

Often out on the grounds we'd see a great cloud of smoke rising from the water, and I'd shout to Vady that there was a boat on fire, but he never shared my excitement. "Keep calm," he'd say, "it's only the *Dare Devil,* and she's not on fire. But circle around her to make sure if you like." I'd make the circle, and, sure enough, it was only the exhaust of her one-cylinder motor, sending out a column of steam like a locomotive on a heavy grade.

Their arrangements were for Gid to furnish the brains and most of the brawn. They would divide the money after deducting expenses. It seemed satisfactory. Gid wasn't afraid of work, and he loved to fish. They were getting their share of fish, doing better than most of us, often coming in with hundred-dollar loads. Gid always unloaded and received the money, with Old Soot standing by watching the proceedings with a sour face. Then, with Old Soot at his heels, Gid would do the evening shopping, carefully folding up the store slip Gladys gave him and putting it in his pocket with the fish money.

Back on the boat it was Gid's chore to store the groceries away in the tiny locker, then clean up the boat, a job he accomplished with very little effort as it consisted mostly of sloshing a pail or two of salt water in the checkers.

This done, and with Old Soot still trailing him, he'd go below, take down the cigar box that held their grocery and fish slips, and get out the little account book he kept there.

"What's that you're writin' now?" Old Soot would ask as Gid copied off the grocery items.

"Expenses," Gid would answer, scratching busily away.

"What you puttin' down now?" Soot would whine, peering nearsightedly over Gid's shoulder. "Can't see wuth a damn tonight, with that sun on the water all day."

"Income," Gid would say.

"What you doin' now?" as Gid took out the money and arranged it in two piles on the dirty bunk.

"That's it," Gid would say, handing the account book to Old Soot. "This one's expenses. This one's shares," pointing out the two piles of money.

Old Soot made quite a ritual of the evening's tally. First he had to find his glasses. It took quite a while as he stirred around through all the odds and ends in the galley. But at last, with the steel bows tucked behind his ears, he'd drop down on the bunk and run a dirty finger down the figures, nodding sagely now and then.

The next step in the night's performance took some prodding on Gid's part. When Old Soot had finally laid down the book, Gid would hand him the share money, but Soot never seemed to be in a hurry about dividing it. "You sure about them accounts?" he'd ask.

"You saw them. If you're not satisfied do it yourself."

At that Old Soot would grunt and hand out the money one-for-you-and-one-for-me.

The evening the *Dare Devil* came in with a hundred-sixty-dollar load, Gid was hilarious with joy. Old Soot watched the unloading with a frown. He hitched up his pants, scratched under his arms, and stamped around the deck. It was plain to see he was in a bad mood.

When they were unloaded they tied to the *Emblem*. Soon we heard loud voices. "Where's my glasses?" Old Soot shouted. "You've hid 'em on me!"

"On your nose, you damned fool!" Gid yelled back.

There were scuffling sounds and then a crash. Gid bounded up the narrow stairs and lit on the deck in one jump. The account book whistled past his head, missing it by inches.

Old Soot was right behind, his face livid with rage. "Git to hell out of here!" he screamed. "We're through! All summer you've been stickin' that cockeyed book under my nose. You know damned well I can't read!"

The next day Gid went back to Hydaburg on one of the seine boats, the end of a beautiful friendship.

The *Dobbs,* a "married boat," so called because the troller's wife fished with him, had been named with startling originality, for the name of the family on it was Dobbs; Mr. and Mrs. and "Sonny," age ten. We never learned their given names, in a country where so few are ever called by their surnames. Mrs. called him Dobbs and so did everyone else except Sonny, who called him Paw. Mrs. was Mrs. Dobbs to everyone except her husband, to whom she was "the missus." They were from some little town between Tacoma and Bremerton, and made the round trip to Alaska every year in their boat.

Mrs. Dobbs was a frail-looking little thing, and one of the few women I ever saw who wore housedresses out on the fishing grounds. Dobbs did all the shopping and we caught only occasional glimpses of her when she'd come out on deck to hang up a few pieces of washing or do some other household chore.

Dobbs suggested a Tinkertoy, as if he'd been hung together with wire loops. When he walked his legs seemed to fold up in a loose-jointed sort of way, then snap out straight as he took a step. His shoulders hung to one side, as if a wire had come unfastened, and his head bobbed around in a disconnected manner.

If his dad was looped together with wire, then Sonny had inherited something from him, at least. I could have sworn he was made of wire springs. He was everywhere at once. One minute he'd be climbing the mast of the *Bluebird* and the next we'd see him running around the trap logs like a lizard. If I turned around suddenly to step back on the *Emblem,* he'd be right under my feet, but before I could move he'd skitter away and some fisherman would be yelling, "Hey, there! Get out of my spoon bucket!" Sonny had energy.

Dobbs was always in evidence too. In fact there was seldom a time when the *Dobbs* was tied to the fish trap that his high-pitched nasal twang couldn't be heard all over the bight. He was in Alaska for "what I can get out of 'er, by God. She's a rich country, and I'm goin' to get my share."

Several times during the summer we heard him tell how he'd found a halibut nursery in the spring. "Them halibut were all under legal size for sellin', but their livers weren't, and I'll be damned if I'm throwin' away livers at a dollar ninety a pound. They's plenty more halibut comin' on to eatin' size. I ain't so dumb to throw the little bastards back with their livers in 'em. Nobody ain't goin' t' ketch me, no how."

Sonny listened to this tale with unfailing joy. "Paw coulda' retired after that trip," he added proudly, "but we ain't ready to retire yet, are we, Paw? Paw's teachin' me some tricks. We're goin'—"

"Shut up! Go tell your maw to get dinner on the table."

The first time Johnny Grayson heard the story he sidled over beside Vady and plucked at his sleeve. "Say," he whispered, "did that fellow say a dollar ninety a pound for halibut liver?"

"That's right. That's what it's bringing now."

"Oh, my gosh!" Johnny said in awe. "I must have ate two dollars' worth of liver for breakfast this morning."

For Johnny that was an expensive breakfast. The largest load we saw him bring in all summer was fifteen cohos. He was an anemic-looking little fellow, a sort of yellowish tan with light ocher hair, eyebrows, and tiny mustache, and a skin the same color but about half a shade darker. He worked in a laundry in Ketchikan during the winter, so perhaps that was why he looked so faded.

Johnny was a great sleeve plucker, if not much of a fisherman. He took a liking to Vady and was always following him around plucking at his sleeve to attract attention. He looked vaguely familiar but I couldn't remember why until the night, after he'd done his evening shopping, I saw him stumble across the deck of the *Dobbs* to his own boat. As he backed out and headed toward the fish traps to tie up, I did some excited sleeve-plucking myself. "Vady, look! Johnny's that fellow we were talking to in Thomas Basin! That boat is *Stinky*—I mean, *My Chance!*"

Clyde filled us in on Johnny's home life. It seems his Indian wife was a "bar fly," and she gave him a bad time. She was about three times as heavy as Johnny, and he wasn't the aggressive type anyway. If he didn't fork over his pay check, she'd rough him up a bit. He'd been known to appear at work with a black eye the day after payday. Going out to the fishing grounds for the summer gave him a chance to get healed up, ready for the winter's mauling.

Vady knew most of the fishermen, by sight, at least. He should have, after all the hours he'd spent in Thomas Basin. I soon noticed that while he talked to most of the fishermen he never had much to say to Flick Greer on the *Taku Wind.* It surprised me, but when I mentioned it he said he wasn't avoiding Flick, it was just that he didn't have anything to talk to him about.

Flick, a charter member of the newly formed Fisherman's Union, had taken it upon himself to bring law and order to the fishing grounds. Being radical and hot-headed, he translated the bylaws of the union to suit himself and often stirred up hard feelings and discontent among the other fishermen.

We'd known Flick and his wife, Dorothy, slightly in Ketchikan. We'd met them at the home of mutual friends and they seemed like a nice couple. Dorothy usually fished with her husband, but this summer she was staying home with a new baby. I soon noticed that Flick's manner was rather overbearing, as if he felt he was a little better than the rest of the fishermen. He and Dobbs argued every night over some technicality of fishing, but one night they had it hot and heavy.

Flick had seen Dobbs shoot a halibut that day out on the grounds and he was boiling mad. All of us caught halibut at times, but as it was out of season for them by this time and against the law to sell them, we tried to turn them loose with as little damage as possible.

"What's the idea of killing halibut?" he said to Dobbs as the *Dobbs* came up to the *Bluebird* to unload. "I saw you shoot one today. A guy like you ought to be kicked out of Alaska or busted one in the jaw."

"If you think I'm lettin' a halibut get away with a dollar spoon you're crazy," Dobbs said.

"It's guys like you that make fishing a tough racket for us honest men," Flick blustered, jumping off his boat and climbing onto the *Bluebird,* where he could glare down on Dobbs. "Why, I've even seen you fishing Behm Canal after the area was closed."

"Where was you if you saw me in Behm Canal?" Dobbs asked. "Mind, I ain't sayin' you did. Why don't you mind your own . . ." Dobbs's face was getting red as he followed Flick up to the *Bluebird*'s deck.

"Don't you tell me to mind my business," shouted Flick. "It's the business of every union fisherman on the grounds to see that the laws are obeyed. We fought for 'em and they're for the protection of us all. No dirty scab's going to tell me off!" He made a menacing move toward Dobbs and began peeling off his coat.

"Don't call me a scab," Dobbs yelled, yanking at the sleeve of his oilskin jacket. "If I don't belong to your damned union that's my business. This here's a free country, and no trap robber's goin' tell me I have to join!"

"Simmer down, you fellows." Leo Dirks, skipper of the *Bluebird*, stepped between them. "We're not going to have any fighting here. Go onto your own boats or onshore to do your arguing. I can't weigh fish with this fighting going on every night, and there are ladies here. Gladys is trying to figure fish slips."

"I'll see you later," Flick said, jumping down onto the deck of the *Taku Wind*. He started the motor and went out into the bay to anchor as he always did, well away from the other boats.

"You're damned right you will," Dobbs shouted as he picked up his pew and began unloading his fish.

"Forty-six pounds of reds," Leo read from the scales, "get that, Gladys?"

"Forty-six," Gladys repeated, making a note of it. She was a whiz at figures and we never knew of her making a mistake on a fish slip. That took a level head with all the noise and confusion going on during the unloading. She was the wife of Jeff, the mate on the *Bluebird*, and had come up from Seattle to join him for what she thought was to be a summer's vacation on the water. She soon found herself with a full-time job, cooking for the crew, figuring the fish slips, paying off the fishermen, and taking care of supplies. The galley of the *Bluebird* was full of boxes, crates, cases and sacks of canned goods, fishing gear, bread, vegetables, and whatever else in the way of supplies the fishermen needed. Even the six bunks were piled high. Just the selling was enough work for one person, as she usually had to move boxes and bags to find what was wanted. Whenever there was a pause in the fish buying, she had to go down the steep ladder to the galley and stand patiently by while some fisherman did his shopping, trying to make up his mind whether he'd have a can of pears or apricots for his supper.

No sooner was she down in the galley than Jeff would call from the hold where he was icing fish, "Oh, Gladys! Fish!"

At that she'd have to hurry the fisherman tactfully into making his decision of "after all I guess I'll take peaches." Then she'd climb back up the ladder, take her place at her improvised apple-box desk, and resume her bookkeeping.

I didn't envy Gladys. Especially I didn't envy her when the *Arrow* came in. Why the Batchelors had ever decided to be fishermen we couldn't understand. They didn't look like fishermen or act like fishermen. He looked like a worn-out shoe clerk and talked like an impressionable tourist just back from England. She looked as if her parents had been stingy with food, and talked as if she had learned a good lesson from them.

As Leo weighed their fish they watched every move, Mrs. Batchelor standing close to his elbow to compare his weights with those she had written on a pad. They kept a small scale on their boat, weighing each fish carefully when it was caught and again when it was dressed, keeping track of the weights down to the half and quarter pounds. This was quite unnecessary, as Leo always gave us the benefit of the fraction in poundage.

On good nights Mr. Batchelor tossed "Bah Joves" around as easily as he flicked his Egg Wobbler into the water every morning. On bad nights his version of English had a hillbilly twang, punctuated with profanity. Strangely, he was a good fisherman, one of the best, although his fish looked as if he'd walked on them—soft, and with the scales knocked off.

"It's just a lark to me," Mrs. Batchelor would squeal, her gimlet eyes watching the scale. "Oh, Leo, you naughty boy, that one must weigh more than ten pounds. See here, I have it down as a big red," flashing the pad.

"See for yourself," Leo would say, turning the face of the scale for her to read.

"Well," grudgingly, "I suppose you're right, but are you sure those scales are accurate? I know we were short-weighed last night. You see"—and she'd glance coyly around at the watching fishermen—"I only want what's coming to us. How much did our liver weigh, Leo?"

"Two ounces!" Leo's voice was grim.

"Are you sure you didn't weigh one of our reds as a white? We don't want to make mistakes, do we?" with a smirk.

"You stood right here and watched me," Leo said. "They're in the hold now. We can't sort your fish out of the pile once they're weighed in."

She never appeared satisfied. She'd argue over a white salmon, which brought a few cents less a pound, and for the three-cents-a-pound difference between a small red or a large, over twelve pounds, she would hold up the other fishermen for ten or fifteen minutes.

No matter how many boats were waiting to unload, Gladys had to leave her station on deck and go below while Mrs. Batchelor did her evening shopping. Her voice carried up the ladder to the impatient fishermen.

"Is that the only brand of coffee you have, dear? I don't think we can use that. Do you have canned artichokes?

Strawberries? Bananas? Oh, bother, what on earth shall we eat? I wish you'd try to get more variety, dear. Well, give us a small can of those beans. Thirty-five cents! That's robbery! I got the very same thing in Ketchikan for thirty-two. You folks must be making a good little thing off of us poor fishermen."

If I had been Gladys, I would have stuffed the beans down her throat, can and all, but Gladys was always pleasant and patient. We learned later that Gladys didn't get a thing for her summer's work except her board and room. The owner of the boat argued that he hadn't asked her to come up from the States, and he made it stick.

The afterdeck of the *Bluebird* was stacked with fifty-gallon drums of gas that had to be pumped into the boats by hand, a task for the fisherman and the *Bluebird's* crew after the fish had been weighed in.

About every four days, or oftener if the fish were plentiful, the packer had to make the eighty-mile run to Ketchikan with the load. These trips were usually made at night after the evening buying, and in every kind of weather. Arriving in Ketchikan early in the morning, the *Bluebird* would unload the fish, which were iced in the hold, at the cold-storage and take on new ice. Groceries, vegetables, and meat were loaded from another wharf. While this was going on Gladys would be uptown taking care of the errands for the fishermen and getting the mail. Wooden-Wheel Johnson needed a belt pulley. Shorty's request, "Mind dropping in at Ellis Air Lines to see if my package came up from the States yet?", necessitated her taking a taxi, as there wasn't time to waste in walking. "Call my wife while you're in and tell her to send out some clean clothes next trip," Johnny had yelled as the *Bluebird* pulled out. Poor Gladys! By the time they were ready to leave she was as frazzled as last year's mooring line. One more stop, at the oil dock for gas and oil, and the *Bluebird* was on her way back to Kaigani to arrive in time to buy fish in the evening. It was a grueling schedule.

Chapter 14

Fishermen are not a dressy lot at any time, and as the season progressed, clothes that had been "good enough for fishing" wore thin at elbows and knees. Without access to barbers the men's hair grew long and out of bounds. Some had curls that swept up over their ears and crinkled along coat collars; some had strands that hung straight beneath their caps or stood up like freshly shaken dust mops. The women, without the aid of beauty parlors, had like difficulties. Permanents straightened out, and pigtails and bandannas hid the evidence that not all women are born with curly hair. Skins became rough and weather-beaten. As we all showed signs of wear, there was no cause for embarrassment.

Vady was out with the earliest. Occasionally I'd get up when he did, just to watch the boats leave the harbor. It was a sight both impressive and stirring—the parade of the fishing fleet.

As the first pink rays of the sun lowered over the hilltops, one boat after another showed signs of waking from its short summer nap. Wispy gray smoke spiraled reluctantly from cold stoves. There was a sharp staccato beat of motors warming up for their long day on the water. Sleepy fishermen came out on deck, like moles from their burrows, rubbing their eyes clear of sleep to size up the weather. One by one lines were coiled on deck and boats backed away from the traps, heading out of the harbor, leaving the calm waters of the bight ruffled by their V-shaped wakes.

At that time each boat seemed to have a personality of its own. Some, eager for the day's adventure, charged out of the harbor like spirited horses, white manes flying. Others dawdled along, their engines spluttering—cross children, half awake. The *Skookum* was a ballet dancer, graceful and light; the *Emblem* a fat old lady, waddling to market.

Usually, although it was impossible to sleep once the Diesel began clanging, I'd lie in the bunk until Vady had the lines out. It was an idea of his that had my hearty approval. There was really no need for me to get up, as he could steer the boat from the cockpit. I'd make breakfast and yell up that his "little darlings," his name for the morning hot cakes, were ready, then go up to watch the poles while he ate. Often I had to call him away from his meal to pull fish.

On days when the water was calm and the sun shone, I'd tell myself what a wonderful thing it was to have a husband who wanted me with him. Then he'd complain of the bright sun. "How I hate this sunshine! I wish it would cloud up and rain so a person could fish in comfort." Strangely enough, he meant it, for his skin is as tender as a baby's and sunburns as readily. Before the summer was over we learned a way to combat it. A thick layer of cold cream followed by pancake make-up, while it gave him the appearance of an Apache painted up for a war dance, protected his face better than anything else.

On cloudy days, when the water was lumpy and the feel of rain was in the air, he'd be happy as a bird in spring. I, depressed by the dark weather and hint of winds to come, would grumble to myself that "Any man who would take his wife out on a tiny fishing boat is something less than human."

While we fished Cape Muzon we usually stayed in the lee of the point, close to the rocks, hoping for kings. But on days when I felt venturesome we'd try out beyond in the tide rips. There the *Emblem* was at her worst. With the swells from the ocean coming in against the tide, the waves built up into high peaks that tumbled in every direction. Creeping slowly along, the boat groaned and twisted. She'd stay in the same place for what seemed like hours, engine chugging, while I watched some object on shore to check our progress. Seeing we weren't moving, or perhaps were slipping backward, I'd advance the throttle. Then Vady's voice would boom out from the cockpit, "For gosh sake, what are you doing now? Slow down! Can't you see the lines are stringing out straight behind?" Sure, I could see it. Who couldn't? But I wanted to get out of there. Then it was chug, chug, chug, for another hour or so.

Around the cape where the swift current swirled and eddied, the water was full of activity. Hundreds of herring and sea bass and occasionally a salmon jumped and floundered about, feeding on smaller fish. Gulls screamed and circled overhead; eagles soared and swooped down to snatch a fish and carry it off to some lofty treetop. Ducks of several varieties, sea parrots, and shags all added to the clamor as they rushed in from all directions to the dining table.

Why a king, that fishy monarch, should want to skulk beneath some overhanging ledge, or feed along the rocks of a point, is beyond me. In my ignorance of the habits of fish I had thought we would find them well out from shore, in deep water free from hazards. I learned to my sorrow, through a summer course of shouted orders, that such is not the case.

"Make an inside turn. Maybe we can pick up a king," Vady would demand about once every hour.

"I can't. We're too close to shore now!"

"Yes, you can!" emphatically. "There's lots of room. Go on! Turn!"

Those inside turns! How I dreaded them.

We'd never make it! I knew we'd never make it! How could I swing the *Emblem* into that tight place, miss that log, dodge that boat, and not tangle the lines?

He'd yell again from the cockpit, but I wouldn't stick my head out the door. I knew too well what he was saying.

"All right, old man, you asked for it," I'd grumble, then take my spite out on the wheel with a vicious yank. Sometimes it worked. We even caught kings that way, but it was the times we got into trouble that gave me the most satisfaction—when Vady had to unknot tangled lines. I kept hoping he'd finally learn I had some judgment about those turns.

Reaching the protection of the lee of the point at last,

I'd squeeze in as close to the shore as I dared, crowding the boats already there to get into calm water. Many dirty looks were directed toward me on that drag, but by night, while we waited to unload at the *Bluebird,* the very fishermen I had crowded would kid us good-naturedly about it.

We often saw sea lions and seals. Sometimes we'd catch fleeting glimpses of a sharp black fin as a shark came close to the surface. One day we hooked a mud shark. Vady had pulled three cohos in succession that were badly chewed. His next strike was such a vicious one we were sure he had a king. The gurdy squealed as he pulled it in. No wonder! When he grasped the leader, a shark on the other end, three feet away, stared him in the eye, our fish crosswise in its mouth. Those cold green eyes were malignant; its teeth looked sharp enough and long enough to bite off an arm. I heard Vady's exclamation of surprise and saw his eyes bug out, but before I could run out to the cockpit it had broken the leader and was gone.

"How large was it?" I asked.

"Big as a submarine," Vady said in awe, his eyes still wide.

"Oh, come now, how big was it really?"

"About twelve feet," he admitted, "but an awfully long twelve feet."

After an hour or so of this kind of tumult I would be as exhausted as if I too had been battling the swift currents. It was worse than a day at the county fair. Possibly it was because of the difficulty of keeping my footing and fighting the *Emblem,* but more, I think, from the excitement of all that frantic activity.

By this time I had quite a good opinion of my ability to keep the *Emblem* in the fish. Wasn't I the one who had seen the cohos finning in the mouth of the harbor so thick we could have cut a chunk out of the water and fried it for supper? Was it my fault when we went around and around for an hour and never had a strike?

If there is anyone living who thinks life on a troller is one long, lazy summer vacation, I'd like to get in touch with him. I have my own opinions on the matter. Sometimes I'd recall Vady's remark of early spring, quote: "You won't have anything to do but steer the boat and order the crew around . . ." Unquote. And paint!

Ho hum! To find, after all these years, that I was married to a man so careless with the truth. Oh yes, I steered the boat! I also prepared most of the meals, polished spoons, washed our clothes, and tried unsuccessfully to keep the galley clean, all under conditions that wouldn't be tolerated in any home.

As for painting! Occasionally, struck by the beauty all around us, I'd make a quick, wobbly sketch, with my pad balanced on the wheel, while I kept a sharp lookout for kelp, logs, and other boats and watched the tips of four poles.

Being the coward I am about the water, I spent most of my days worrying about future storms, or storms that seemed to be making up at the moment. I watched the gulls until they must have felt they had no privacy at all. If one soared, I tried to ignore it, but when several spiraled up into the sky, wheeling and gliding with wings outspread, I tried to think of a good excuse to hurry into the harbor, for during a blow the gulls always soar.

Don't get the impression that I didn't enjoy the summer in my own peculiar way. How could it have been otherwise with a companion as enthusiastic as mine? His sense of humor never failed. He was always ready to see the funny side to some of our most trying experiences, and he was having a wonderful time.

It was interesting fishing with so many boats. Having a partner made me feel as if we belonged, although we didn't see much of Nina and Clyde. We could seldom tie together in the evening and we usually beat them out in the morning.

When we passed them on the grounds Vady would hail them. "Hi, Clyde, how many fish you got?"

Clyde would hold up his hand, spreading his fingers to show their catch, and call back, "You doing anything?"

We might have more or we might have none at all, but invariably Vady would double Clyde's report.

"Why did you say that?" I'd remonstrate. "You told him twenty. You know darned well we have only seven. We'll have to stay out until we get thirteen more if it takes all night."

"Makes me feel good to hear I'm such a good fisherman," Vady would say, grinning. Then, "Watch out there! Look where you're going!"

Now that the little interchange of fishing news was over, Nina and I would return to our wheels. She never seemed to realize how far behind the boat the lines dragged. She'd cut across our bow, giving me a bad time as I maneuvered the *Emblem* into a quick turn to keep from crossing their lines.

Vady was a noisy fisherman, yelling when he landed a big one, pounding the deck with the gaff when one got away, or, if in his hurry he threw it clear across the deck and jerked it off the hook, he'd see it swim away. When we passed other boats he'd shout at them, something that sounded like, "I'd boo ye ack ig gale cover bear yong byland?"

"What's that?" the puzzled fisherman would call back.

"Ig bedection shrift," Vady would yell, gesticulating wildly, "bagging aground ber boat."

By that time the poor fisherman, almost out of earshot, would be checking over his boat, wondering what in the world was wrong. Vady would give him a cheerful wave and go back to fishing. It embarrassed me, but Vady thought it was great fun.

He rooted and cheered when the other fishermen landed a big one. "You're the noisiest fisherman I ever heard," I told him. "You don't hear anyone else going on like that."

"I can't help what they do. Those guys take themselves too seriously. I came out for a good time, and by golly, I'm having it!" For proof he'd break into song, off key, out of tune, but loud.

Early in the year we'd found how useless it was to try to carry on a conversation between the cockpit and the pilothouse. With the Diesel throbbing under my feet I could hear him only when he yelled. I wasn't used to that. He doesn't raise his voice even in an argument. It led to misunderstandings. I'd take his directions to mean something else and when he'd repeat them in a shout I'd think he was angry. He, on his part, thought I was purposely going against his wishes. I wondered whether I'd develop cauliflower ears from the constant impact of those shouted orders.

Westerly winds were common, usually springing up early in the afternoon. Then the trollers fished inside the cape along the shore line, which was steep-to with good depths. Late in the afternoon fog from the ocean rolled over the mountaintop, cascading like a huge waterfall, dissipating halfway down the mountainside in the warm air from the land.

The seine boats, having the advantage of size, often stayed out beyond the cape after the trollers came inside. All but the *Mermaid*, owned by Nat Jones, a Haida Indian. Nat was a huge brown mountain of a man, who fished naked except for a pair of dirty trunks. He had two grandsons aboard, lads of twelve and thirteen who did the fishing while Nat sat on the afterdeck in a straight-backed chair, his fat paunch glistening in the sun. Nat hadn't gone to the trouble of putting on trolling poles or gurdies. There wasn't even a rail around the deck. The boys hauled the fish hand over hand, slinging them on deck with a jerk that often sent them slithering across and off the other side. This brought forth yells of delight from the boys, while Nat sat there tipping his chair back on two legs and laughing in belly-shaking roars.

At first I'd been hurt by the unfriendly attitude of the fishermen. Being a woman, I have the privilege of changing my mind. Now I was impressed by the spirit of friendliness and co-operation.

There are limits beyond which a fisherman can be neither coerced nor cajoled into talking. Ask one what bait he is using, which spoons are best, where he made that big catch yesterday, or any of a number of trade secrets, and he'll clam up and leave you talking to yourself. But run a hook through your thumb, burn out a bearing, or be in need of some tool, and nine out of ten fishermen will go to endless trouble to help you.

We became seasoned enough that summer to understand their attitude, for we had a secret too. It was one of my duties to keep a fishing log. When we caught a fish I'd jot down the time of day, spoon used, and the stage of the tide. This log proved valuable. It was by referring to it that Vady discovered the possibilities of our "hole."

A certain place (secret, of course) had proved to be lively fishing during the two hours before slack tide. It was by accident that Vady discovered its true worth. I went below to read, and while I was gone he experimented.

With all the glee of a small boy snitching a jar of jam he ran into such a constricted passage between the rocks that when I came on deck I couldn't believe we were still afloat. He gave me directions for negotiating a tricky figure eight that took us over his newly discovered fishing grounds.

"Down past the rocks. Close, but not too close. Swing out to avoid that reef. Turn as near to that kelp-covered rock as you can. Now, out into the channel to turn, but not too far or you'll be out of the fish."

When I got the hang of it, it was great fun, for we could tell almost to the exact spot when to expect a strike. Each time around I became more daring until Vady, looking up during a quiet interval, cried out in alarm, "You don't have to beach the boat, you know!" I *was* shaving it pretty close.

At high tide the fish stopped biting as suddenly as if they had been feeding by a stop watch. But from that day on we caught from twenty to forty cohos during that two-hour period. It upped our catch to such a gratifying total that the other fishermen marveled at what they called "Eberhart's luck."

Because Vady fished close to the bottom we caught more ling cod than most of the fishermen. When we dragged them in, their enormous heads half out of water, eyes popping, huge mouths wide open with tongues hanging out, they looked like an evolutionary error. Seeing us unload them at night, the fishermen nicknamed our boat the *Alligator Express.*

The evening routine seldom varied. Unload and weigh in our catch, receive our fish slip, which Gladys cashed at once, do our shopping. Then, while Vady cleaned the boat and gassed up, I'd prepare supper.

That was a restful meal, the one meal of the day when we could take our time. Tired and relaxed, we dawdled over it as we discussed the day's adventures and decided on tomorrow's fishing grounds. Vady would take out his wallet to count our hundred-dollar bills—our stake for the future—while I counted the coins in the fish jar, saved for the day when we could exchange them for another bill to add to our growing pile.

All the fishermen had fish jars and kept their money on the boats all season. At first I thought that risky, but there was no pilfering on the boats, even when a fisherman went to town on the plane and left his boat unlocked in the harbor for several days.

Chapter 15

Our Diesel had been behaving so well since we left Ketchikan it almost seemed Vady had been right in thinking we'd have no more trouble. Then, one evening as we were coming in, the usual clattering, followed by silence, told us there was trouble ahead. The *Skookum* was nowhere in sight. We hadn't seen her all day. The other boats were coming in, so I tied a towel to the boom. Soon Dobbs saw us and towed us into the harbor. Once inside and tied up, he came aboard and spent the entire evening working with Vady over the motor, trying to locate the trouble–losing sleep he needed badly.

When Vady offered to pay him he exploded in a profane refusal. "Hell, no! Why, damn it, man, you'd help me, wouldn't you? Ain't we all fishin' together, tryin' to make a livin'?"

Right then I began to have a soft spot in my heart for Dobbs, crooked as we knew him to be.

Vady was optimistic when we went to bed. "It's only a broken valve stem," he said. "We have a spare, and it won't take long to slip it in in the morning."

Clyde insisted, next morning, on staying in to help, but they soon found that the stem on the new valve was bent. That meant a trip to Ketchikan for a new one. Clyde immediately offered to take Vady in. Nina was still missing the things she had left behind and was eager for mail from home. So, although it was threatening a southeaster, they left at three that afternoon.

The *Skookum* was a fast boat, too fast for the heavy seas they encountered. The stern dragged down and the waves came over into the cockpit. They had to slow down. Darkness overtook them as they were crossing Clarence Strait in the fog. Then the fuel line plugged. While they were drifting, cleaning it out, they lost their bearings. When daylight came they found they were in a veritable trap of pinnacles and crags.

"Weren't you terribly frightened?" I asked Nina when they returned.

"No, I wasn't frightened at all," she answered. "I slept right through, all the way. I knew they'd know what they were doing."

Oh, for such confidence!

I'd been feeling a little smug about the *Emblem,* remembering how white and gleaming her paint was the day they launched her from the ways. Other boats were dirty from a summer on the water. Coming back from a trip to shore in the skiff, I had the shock of my life. Little streamers of fish gurry hung from the rail. Dried blood and scales freckled her sides. From bow to stern was a streak of black where the oil and soot from the water had settled. In fact, she looked like all the other boats, just a dirty old fishing boat.

When I took a pail of soapsuds and the scrub brush to clean her off, one of the trap watchmen came over to watch me work. He was a Scandinavian and had been a trap watchman for the same company for many years. He spoke such broken English it was hard to follow his stories.

Although the trapping season is short, the life of the two men the law requires on each trap is rugged and beset with danger. The shack where they live is barely large enough for their accommodations—two bunks, a table, and a stove. Even though bolted to the logs of the trap and braced with wires, it's not uncommon for a shack to be washed away during a violent summer storm. The traps are usually placed on prominent points, fully exposed to the elements. The law requires a shack or tent onshore where the watchmen can wait out a storm in safety, but sometimes they wait too long before they leave the trap. It's tricky business to walk out on a heaving log and climb into a skiff, rolling and rocking in a heavy sea. Even if they get into the skiff there's still the dangerous landing on the beach to negotiate, with the pounding surf trying to dash them against the rocks. Hardly a season passes but one or more watchmen lose their lives.

Although every possible safeguard was used by the companies to ensure safe delivery of the fish from traps to canneries, many thousands of fish were illegally sold back to them by the pirates. In spite of spiller covers, a network of steel padlocked into place to be opened only by the tender skippers when they came to brail, two watchmen living on the trap, a patrol boat to watch the watchmen, patrol plane to watch the patrol boat, and company spotters on the tenders, pirating was still a big business.

"You vould be surprised, lady," the watchman told me, "how many of dese boats in dis harbor have contacted me already, and ve ain't yet out on de grounds."

Pirates? In Kaigani! Who could they be? Flick? Of course not. Wasn't he the upholder of law and order? Johnny? Hardly. Not poor little faded Johnny, running from his own shadow. Dobbs? A possibility. My talk with the watchman had given me something to ponder.

Vady had picked up our mail in town, and among other things were two fan letters in praise of my *Alaska Sportsman* covers. Fan letters for me! I could hardly contain myself! Even better was a request from the editor for more paintings!

By the time the motor was repaired we had lost four days of good fishing. Then we had another southeaster, right on the heels of the one that had tailed Clyde and Vady into Ketchikan.

Many of the high-liners, that intrepid group of fishermen who go out in all seasons and every kind of weather, to bring back record catches while back-channel fishermen like ourselves were scratch-fishing, left for grounds farther north during the blow. Usually they carry ice, and, knowing from experience where the fish are most likely to be, they waste no time in getting there. We were satisfied to wait out the storm, as we had been averaging more than fifty dollars a day at Cape Muzon.

Being harbor-bound, we all took advantage of the layover, and there was much activity aboard the boats. Suits of long underwear and other articles of clothing festooned the booms. Pail after pail of water, dirty from the cleaning going on below decks, was dumped back into the bight. There was much visiting between boats. Cakes and pies appeared on galley tables where a hastily opened can of fruit had served as dessert for many weeks.

Some of the fishermen usually gathered in the galley of the *Bluebird* in the evening for a game of poker. I was shocked when Vady suggested I join them.

"Gladys asked me if you wouldn't come," he said. "She's embarrassed being the only woman, and there's no place else for her to go. Mrs. Dobbs wouldn't go and Nina doesn't play cards. Neither do the other women. I told her you'd be glad to."

So I went. It was fun.

I'd never played poker and knew nothing about the game. I couldn't remember the value of the hands and would think I had a sure winner with a pair. I'd bet high and the others, thinking I knew what I was doing, would soon drop out. Those Haida Indians helped us make up for some of our loss while we were unable to fish.

At last it cleared up, a glassy-calm day with bright sunshine. As always in the afternoon I was half dozing at the wheel. I glanced idly out the window and looked straight down into the bewhiskered face of a little old man! He floated just on the surface of the water, eyes closed. I recoiled from the window, feeling the blood drain from my face. Horrified, I forced myself to take another shuddering look. Then I saw it was a sea lion. With his front flippers locked behind his head, his back ones folded neatly on his stomach, he was taking a nap, rocking gently in the arms of the ocean. Hearing the throb of the motor, he opened his eyes, looking more than ever like a grizzled old veteran. Up came the flippers! With a splash he was gone. The memory of that little sleeping face stayed with me for a long while, the resemblance to a corpse had been so real.

Unknowingly Nina let me in for a bad time. We passed the *Skookum* and she was pulling a fish. Clyde was nowhere in sight.

"That's the kind of a wife for me," Vady said, "one who can fish."

That did it! He'd hinted often enough that I should learn to fish. I slammed out of the pilothouse. "Get over!" I snapped, crawling into the cockpit. "I'll fish if I lose an arm."

"This is more like it," Vady said, pulling in a fish. He gaffed it and swung it toward the checker. It smacked me across the back of the neck and fell to the deck. "I knew you'd enjoy it if I could ever get you out here."

He picked up the knife, reached for the fish, and began to clean it.

"I'm getting this down to a science," he said. "When we first came out it took me a minute to clean a fish. Now I can clean three in a minute and do a better job." The knife flashed busily. Bits of blood, slime, and gurry hit me in the face and stuck to my jacket. The smell was sickening.

"I've always thought if you're going to do something, learn to do it right. Lots of these dudes follow along the same lines all their lives, never try to improve their methods." He took the fish by the gills and dipped it over the side to wash it. He threw it into the checker and I got a shower of slimy water. He picked up another. "They go on year after year, using the same spoons, afraid to—You've got a fish! Pull it in!"

"I can't. You pull it."

"Go ahead, pull it in, you'll never learn if you don't try."

He went back to his cleaning.

I threw in the gurdy. The fish came in willingly. I landed it without mishap.

"Gee, that's easy!" I boasted. "There's really nothing to it, is there?"

I picked up a spoon and gave it a heave that sent it far out onto the water. It sank from sight. I'd neglected to snap it onto the line. I glanced quickly at Vady. He hadn't noticed. I picked up another and snapped it on. I began letting out the line. There was a jerk and the line hung limp.

"Something the matter here," I said.

Vady felt the line. "You've snapped off the lead," he said. "I told you to hold it and ease it down gently. We might as well go in. I'll have to buy a new lead. No, I'll tell you what we'll do. We'll go into Little Daykoo and spend the afternoon on the beach."

That was something like it! I'd be happy to exchange a lead for an afternoon on the beach.

Little Daykoo Harbor, halfway between Kaigani and Cape Muzon, is a beautiful place. We went in through water so clear we could see the clamshells on the bottom. Beyond the narrow entrance the harbor widened out into a circular bight. At one side the water was deep enough to anchor, shallowing up toward the head.

As we prepared to leave the boat I noticed that the wet gunny sack covering the fish in the checker was partly folded back. I went to the cockpit to straighten it. There at my feet was a salmon heart, beating as busily and rhythmically as if it had not long since been detached from its usual appendages. I'd heard fishermen say a fish heart would beat in the water or on deck for hours. Let me be quoted as saying that ALL those fish had been cleaned for more than half an hour.

We anchored, then, taking the rifle, went ashore in the skiff. At the head of the bight a small creek cut a deep bed through the long flat. Lush grass was waist high. The African plains must be like this, I thought as I strolled along, enjoying the feel of being on land. Good solid earth, soft underfoot. Vady had gone on ahead. I wondered what it would be like to walk through tall grass and suddenly be confronted by a lion. Then I looked down at a patch of sand under my feet. There were fresh tracks, very fresh and very large. Wolf tracks! We must have frightened him when we came in. Beneath them were the tracks of a deer. I looked around and saw Vady, a quarter of a mile away, on the tide flats.

I was starting back to the boat when I heard him yell.

"Come down here," he called. "There's something I want to show you."

Two bears had been there recently. Their tracks covered the flat, and rocks had been turned over where they'd searched for beach crabs at low tide. "They may be right around here close," Vady said. "These tracks are really fresh."

"We may as well go back, then," I said. "I guess that's all we want to see."

"Heck, no. What are you talking about? We were going to spend the afternoon. You're always complaining because we don't go ashore. Come on, we'll take a walk up the creek."

It was a jungle where nature had put every thimbleful of earth to work, not once but many times. Moss, of many varieties, covered the ground. Grasses and vines, trees and bushes grew in the moss. The vines swarmed over small bushes and climbed the tree trunks to tangle among the branches. Down timber and broken stumps, covered with ferns and lichens, littered the forest floor.

Earthy smells of growing plants and rotting wood mingled in the damp air. We followed a trail worn deep through many seasons of use. A bear trail, a succession of deep hollows where each bear had stepped into the footprints of his predecessor.

"I like to think," Vady said in a voice that was barely a whisper, "that I'm the only man who's ever been here. Man-made things and so-called civilization seem so far away I wonder why I ever thought them important. Hear the wind in the treetops? It's like a cathedral, so still, so peaceful."

His deep feeling for the wilderness always surprises me, although I don't know why. I know he loves all nature. Perhaps it was more the surprise of having him disclose his more intimate feelings, something he seldom does.

There was a flash of blue wings, bluer than the patches of sky we glimpsed among the branches. A jay settled on a limb over the creek, uttering his raucous warning to all the forest creatures that strangers were here. A fallen log spanning the creek wore a royal cape of blossoming moss, so red it fairly throbbed in the sunlight.

"Do you suppose the birds and animals enjoy this beauty?" I asked.

"Not unless they can eat it, I guess."

That broke the spell. We started back.

We were nearly to the boat when I looked across the bight. There in a grassy meadow was a bear! No chance of mistaking a bear. Often we'd seen stumps we thought at first glance were bears, but this was no stump! There's nothing in nature so black as the glossy fur of a black bear.

I grabbed Vady's arm and pointed excitedly. The bear was having a wonderful time. Like a happy pig, it wallowed in a mud-filled hollow, lying first on one side then on the other, or on its back with all four feet in the air.

The bight at this point was about three hundred yards across. It is doubtful whether the bear could see us with its notoriously nearsighted eyes. The wind was blowing toward us.

"We'll go around the head of the bight," Vady said softly. "We can sneak in behind those alders and be right on top of him before he knows we're there."

"You can, you mean. I'll go back to the boat. Seems to me I forgot to turn off the stove."

"Fraidy cat," Vady said, grinning. "All right, then, I'll go alone. You can watch me all the way."

The arrangement suited me fine. I hurried back to the boat. From a seat on the stern I had a perfect view. There was Vady, at the head of the bight, working his way down the beach, keeping close to the brush. Sometimes an outcropping of rock had to be passed going down the beach, but a large rocky point made a perfect screen between him and the bear.

The bear, unalarmed, was enjoying the afternoon to the full. Having finished his mud bath, he was drying his fur by pushing himself through the grass on his belly, or rolling over and over. Sometimes he'd stand up, raise up on his hind legs, and sniff the wind, then graze like a horse in the tall beach grass before lying down again.

Vady was close now, coming through the alders, crouching low, his gun ready.

The bear was getting uneasy. He shook his head from side to side. He must have smelled danger as the wind had shifted slightly.

Vady stepped out into the clearing. He stopped and took aim. Then he fired.

It was a good, clean miss.

The bear was off at a lumbering gallop while the echoes of the shot were still ringing in the bight. He was gone in seconds.

Vady loped into the clearing. He walked all around examining the grass, the mud, and the ground, then started back toward the head of the bight.

Now that the bear was frightened away, I'd go back to shore and walk down to meet him. I was halfway to the head of the bight when there was a great crackling in the bushes. A bear burst out, not twenty paces in front of me! It was as big as an elephant! It gave one look in my direction and set off down the beach.

I don't know exactly what happened then. All at once I was in the skiff. Then I was back on the boat. I don't know how I got there, but it was exactly where I wanted to be.

I heard two more shots. Then I waited. After what seemed like a dreadfully long time I saw Vady swinging down the beach. I waited until he was opposite me, then rowed over to get him.

"Did you see that bear? That other bear, I mean. The great BIG one."

"Sure I saw it. Didn't you hear me shoot? It ran right by me. It wasn't a full-grown one. Probably a spring cub, a mangy-looking little thing."

"That was another one, then. It couldn't have been the monster that chased me."

"Now, Babe," Vady laughed, "watch it."

"Anyway, you aren't a very good shot. You missed both of them."

"I wasn't shooting at them," Vady said, to my surprise. "Why would I want to kill them? We couldn't eat that much meat and fishermen are so prejudiced against bear meat they won't touch it."

"I like it."

"You don't like it enough to eat a whole bear, do you?"

"No. But if you weren't even trying to get them, why did you go to so much trouble?"

"I like to hunt."

Chapter 16

Nicknames were common on the fishing grounds, and while it seemed like quite a strain on friendship to hail a man as "Square-Head" or "Buoy-Keg," they never seemed to mind. They wore these names as proudly as if they had been awards of merit.

In fact some of them were. There was Coronation Pete, who earned his "handle" by many years of fishing the dread Coronation Flats. Wooden-Wheel Johnson earned his when he lost his propeller, fashioned one of wood, and it worked!

Then there was Hard-Luck John, whose misfortunes would fill a book, and Muskeg Pete, who'd found that the "cleared land" of his homestead was nothing but barren muskeg bog. And at Kaigani, there was Fourpole.

Fourpole may not have known he had a nickname. He came in one night with an old stamp mill in a squatty little boat that looked as if it had long since earned a rest in some landlocked harbor. He had never owned a sea chart and would have considered it sissy to have one on the boat. Having been born to the water, he relied entirely upon local knowledge. Each day we'd see him fishing far inside the shoal-water mark, and every night someone would ask him, "How many poles did you break today?"

Grinning, he'd hold up his hand, showing one or two fingers.

One night, at the usual question, he spread his hand, showing all but his thumb.

"Four?" they asked incredulously.

"Yep, that's right. Four. All of 'em." And off he went in his skiff to cut down some trees for new poles.

Flick had a dodge he used when someone surprised him in his favorite hole. All fishermen know that when the fish are hitting the fisherman will be busy in the cockpit. So when Flick had unwanted company he'd go into the pilothouse and stay out of sight until his intruder gave up and left, even if there were fish on his lines.

He was stumped the day a troller came along and shouted until Flick came outside, "Hey, you damned cheechako," the fellow called, "why don't you pull your fish? You got something on every cockeyed line!"

Sometimes the fishing-ground humor savored of slapstick and led to discomfort and loss of valuable gear. Johnny Grayson was a beginner who learned the hard way not to believe everything he heard. Enviously he watched Dobbs come in with record loads night after night. He tried following him, but Dobbs eluded him every time. Then one day Johnny found him, fishing in a secluded cove.

"How many fathoms you lettin' down?" Johnny asked trustingly.

"Forty." Dobbs never hesitated over his reply.

Poor Johnny. He lost all his leads and had a broken pole to replace before his faith in Dobbs was shaken.

That night after he'd sold his fish, one coho and two ling cod, he came over to the *Emblem* to tell Vady about it, with the usual sleeve-plucking.

"Why didn't you check up on your chart?" Vady asked. "There isn't a spot in there more than fifteen fathoms deep."

"Now, what would Dobbs tell me that for? How could he have been fishin' forty? You know, Vady, someday I'm going to get me one of them there maps."

But Johnny had good breaks, too, like the day he snagged an entire new stainless-steel line, complete with spoons and rubbers, leaders and leads. Johnny's gear was old, his loot worth many dollars.

"Yes, it was a good-luck find," he admitted, "but I don't like them spoons much. I'd ruther've had other ones, like some of them Superiors. I never catched a strike all day. Superiors are the best spoons I'd ruther have."

Old boats left and new ones came. Sometimes there would be as many as thirty in the harbor, then at a word of a run in another section, many of them would leave. Often the run was over before they reached their destination, so in a few days they'd come dribbling back. That made it very hard for Gladys to estimate the supplies she would need. More often than not there were shortages, especially of meat. It was still hard to get in Ketchikan because of the shipping strike, and there were no facilities for keeping a large supply on the *Bluebird.* One time when she had bought only enough for a few boats, fourteen new ones came in from Chacon. By allowing one package to each boat, she thought, it would give us all a treat.

But Dobbs didn't see it that way. He blustered over to the box where the meat was stacked on ice and filled his arms.

"We can't let you have seven packages of meat, Mr. Dobbs," Gladys explained. "We won't have enough to go around that way. We think all the boats should get a share."

"Well, by God, that's a good one! Ain't I been sellin' you my fish all summer? Ain't I been buying my supplies offen you?"

Of course he had, because it was cheaper for him than making the long run to town, buying his own ice, and losing all that time.

He stood there glowering, his arms full of meat. "I won't say nothin' more, but by Criminy, I'm goin' ta have this meat!"

Rather than have an argument Gladys gave up. You couldn't do much else with a man like Dobbs.

Early the next morning the *Dobbs* left Kaigani, Dobbs shouting his sentiments until they were out of sight. "I'll ice up, by God! I'll sell my fish to white men. The *Bluebird* can go to hell and the crew with it, you ain't gettin' no more of my fish. I'll go to Ketchikan and I'll—"

I'd thought one of the new boats looked familiar when it came in, but I couldn't remember where we'd seen it and I forgot to call Vady's attention to it.

As we passed the entrance to Little Daykoo in the morning on our way to the cape, we saw it high and dry on the sand in the entrance.

Then I remembered! Our friend of McHenry Anchorage.

"Hey," Vady yelled as I kept on going, "don't you see that boat? Turn in!"

"Don't you know who that is?"

"Sure. We've got to see if we can help him."

"That savage?"

"Why, Babe," Vady said, "I'm ashamed of you. Where's your Christian spirit? Of course we'll help him."

But the fellow proved to be as surly over his own misfortune as he'd been over ours. His wasn't very serious anyway, as his boat was sitting in the sand. He said he'd float off when the tide came in, and he did. In a few days he disappeared again, gone to another fishing ground.

Another of the new arrivals from Cape Chacon was a tiny numbered boat, so squat it seemed to have no freeboard at all. Ace and Anna Gunderson were newly married. Ace's mother had come from the States for the wedding and decided to spend the summer with them. We marveled that three grown folks could find places to stand inside, much less live on, so small a boat. They'd had a bad trip from Chacon when their motor, a Diesel about the vintage of ours, had failed and they had drifted in the tide rips for hours while Ace made repairs. The youngsters were fearless. It was their first experience on the water, their first try at fishing. They didn't seem to realize there might be dangers on a boat of that size. Poor Mrs. Gunderson, Sr., was so frightened by their experience she dreaded the arrival of each new day, but she told me with astounding naïveté, "I'm going to stay with them all summer if it kills me. Why, I wouldn't think of spoiling their outing for them by going in and leaving them out here alone!"

Most of the boats were fishing off the cape the day of

the storm. The morning had been beautiful and sunny, but shortly after noon the sky darkened and far out over Dixon Entrance we could see the wind coming. The water was nearly black at the horizon, but nearer we could see great whitecapped breakers rolling toward us. Up went the poles, as quickly as possible, the boats scuttling for safety. Flick, Dobbs, who had come back to Kaigani the day after he left, and Johnny stayed out too long and had to run in behind Little Daykoo Island, where they anchored while the storm blew itself out. When the worst of the blow was over, they had to cross a three-mile stretch of open water to reach the safety of Kaigani Harbor. Johnny's skiff washed overboard, hit against the side of his boat, and broke a plank on the troller.

Dobbs and Flick couldn't do anything to help him in such rough water except slow down and stay with him.

Johnny bailed like a madman and eventually made it in. His boat was leaking so badly he had to put it on the beach, where he worked on it for several days.

It was late evening when we realized the Gundersons were still missing. Someone had seen them at one o'clock, bouncing around in the rips off the cape. Johnny had seen them at two-thirty, standing north on the outside of the island.

The wind had struck about three-thirty.

Old-timers shook their heads. "He'd never make it to the harbor in that gale," Flick said, "not in that pot. She's built too close to the water. One wave over the stern would flood her."

"Get a drop of water on that stamp mill and she's a goner," Square-Head Johnson put in.

"That's a tough old go on the outside," Buoy-Keg added. "I trapped up along the coast one winter and them crags had me scared."

"They might have run in somewhere," Vady said hopefully.

"No place on the outside would be safe," Buoy-Keg told him. "Nothing this side of Security Cove, and that's a good ten miles."

The men gathered in groups, discussing sending out a rescue party. At last the *Bluebird,* the largest boat in the harbor, put out. But she had to come back. The seas at the mouth of the harbor were tremendous.

In the morning, although the seas were still running strong, the boats went out to search. Some of the larger ones, the seine boats, cruised along the outside of the island until the swells drove them back. Others ran close to shore. McLeod Bay, Daykoo and Datzkoo islands, Long Island, and Kaigani Strait all were covered in the hope that the Gundersons might have anchored in one of the harbors. No one found a trace of the missing boat.

A radio message was sent to the Coast Guard in Ketchikan and all day we heard the drone of a circling plane. It landed in the bight in the evening to tell us the search had been fruitless.

For three days there was no fishing at Kaigani. We were all convinced the Gundersons were drowned. Going out in these waters now would be like fishing in a graveyard. It was dusk of the third day when we saw a little boat round the point.

"Looks kinda like the Gundersons' boat," Johnny said.

"Well, it ain't," Flick growled. "You'll never see that boat again."

But it was! The Gundersons seemed surprised that their arrival caused so much commotion.

"Looks like a reception committee," Ace said with an engaging grin, as the men crowded around to help them tie up. "We didn't know we were so popular."

"How are the women? What happened? Where were you? Is the boat all right?" We all crowded around asking questions.

"Why, nothing happened," Ace said, perplexed. "We just went exploring. We had a grand time. A picnic on the beach with roasted weenies, potato salad, cookies, pickles—what else did we have, sweetheart?"

"But the wind! Didn't you take an awful beating? Where did you anchor?"

"It did blow a little, didn't it, sweetheart. But we ran in ahead of it to Security Cove. I had to get up and change the anchor several times that night . . ."

"It was terrible!" his mother moaned.

". . . but the next day was fine. We climbed to a little lake in the hills and slept all afternoon on a grassy bank. It was fun, wasn't it, honey. That night we dug clams and had a beach fire. We roasted the clams over the coals and they opened right up. What else did we do, sweetheart?"

"We came back here today," Anna said shyly. "That was all. We saw a Coast Guard plane flying over Muzon as we came in. It seemed strange to see it so far from Ketchikan."

"It flew so low it almost hit the mast," Mrs. Gunderson put in indignantly. "We could even make out the pilot. He waved to us."

Anna nodded. "I've been wondering why they'd come 'way out here. There doesn't seem much reason for it unless they were searching for someone."

Chapter 17

The fish traps that had been tied in Kaigani were set out in July, one at the cape, the other in McLeod Bay. Trolling was effectively blocked along the shore where we had all done so well during the afternoon westerlies.

By the middle of August most of the boats had left, although fishing was still good in the Cordova Bay area. When Leo told us the *Bluebird* would be leaving soon to pack fish from Ketchikan to Prince Rupert, we knew we would have to find new fishing grounds, much as we disliked the thought.

During the past weeks we had learned the Cordova Bay area well, making several overnight trips to other likely spots nearby. Ruth Bay and the Barrier Islands,

Mabel Bay and Nutkwa, we tried them all with varying success. We anchored in Nina Cove one night when we had to find shelter while Vady cut a great tangled ball of kelp from the propeller. With his fish-cleaning knife tied securely to a long pole, he hacked away at the tough, rubbery whips for several hours before he could get them off. While he was working on it, I took the skiff and explored the little cove from end to end.

We fished Breezy Bay with Nina and Clyde one day when it was too windy to fish off the cape. We found out by evening that we had made a mistake in coming. Following my usual custom, I read the description of the bay as we approached. "It is divided into two arms; there are several islands and numerous rocks in the bay. It does not appear to afford an anchorage." Fishing proved to be poor, and by evening the wind had increased, making the long trip back to Kaigani impractical. We anchored behind a low, rocky point, which was considered fair anchorage during good weather, and tied the boats together. Breezy Bay had been rightly named! Williwaws howled and buffeted the boats all night while Vady and Clyde took turns at anchor watch. If we'd only known, there was a snug little harbor less than two miles away where old-timers took refuge during storms!

We explored many harbors and inlets that were new to us, and some of the uncharted ones Vady wanted to show me. At night when Nina and Clyde were with us, we'd tie the boats together, combine our dinners, and spend a sociable evening on one of the boats.

If we anchored up early when we were alone, we'd take our little skiff with its one-horsepower kicker and cruise along the beach, coming back at dark for a late supper.

Vady was just getting the skiff overside one evening

when he saw a black bear grazing in the long beach grass.

"Hello, old bear," Vady shouted.

The bear lifted his head, sniffed, gazed toward us with his beady, myopic eyes, and went back to feeding. It's doubtful whether he saw us, as we were well out from shore.

"Hi, bear," Vady yelled again. The bear paid no attention. The grass was sweet and succulent. If he heard us he must have felt dinner was more important.

We got into the skiff and were nearly to the beach before he saw us and scrambled off into the woods.

Around the next point we shut off the motor to drift while we watched a gray water ouzel, dipping and bobbing among the boulders of a gurgling mountain stream.

We'd been there only a few moments when a half-grown cub burst out of the bushes, waded out into the creek, and sat down. He looked so comical, so inquisitive, and so happy it was all we could do to keep from laughing aloud. The bushes rustled, and there was mamma bear, brown, and much larger than "old bear." She waded into the creek and gave him a cuff that sent him sprawling. Apparently it wasn't bath night for Junior, or Mamma was afraid he'd take cold. He whimpered his displeasure, walked ashore, and shook himself. Mamma continued down to the beach, turning over rocks and sniffling among the piled-up drift. Junior, making a nuisance of himself, was right under her feet, beating her to every tidbit she uncovered in her hunt.

We were drifting too close to the beach for my peace of mind, although the bears hadn't noticed us. I motioned to Vady to start the motor. At the sound Mamma looked up with a "w-o-o-f." Junior started up a small spruce tree and was promptly knocked out of it by a brown paw as Mamma herded him, howling, back into the woods.

Although the mother bear was brown, she was a black bear. Black bear refers to a species rather than a color and may be any shade from a rather light brown to a rich, glossy black.

As long as the *Bluebird* was leaving and we had to find new fishing grounds, Vady suggested we go to Ketchikan and ice up, making week-long trips to some of the grounds closer home. But when Clyde said he'd like to try the fishing farther north, Vady agreed readily enough.

We left one morning at four o'clock. Ten miles out the usual thing happened—motor trouble. I was still in the bunk when the engine stopped. I heard Vady calling to Clyde from the deck.

"That must be the boulder over there that shows on the chart, or do you think it's that one to starboard? We'd better get our bearings right, there's a reef makes out from shore in here close. Think you can get a line over? Swing close when you turn. There's a submerged rock somewhere off that island, on the port side."

Howkan Narrows!

How jolly! Rocks, more rocks, submerged rocks, and a reef. All that, and the motor sulking. I jumped out of the bunk. What? No kelp? No breakers? I wondered as I dressed. When I went on deck I saw there was kelp, plenty of it, growing in the shoal water all around us. Fortunately the water was calm.

With the towing line secured to the *Skookum,* Clyde towed us through the crooked passage.

Safely through the narrows, Vady called my attention to a bleached totem pole standing on a tiny island to our right.

"Next time we're up this way we'll anchor up, take the

skiff, and go ashore. It looks interesting." Later in the summer we did. The totem, an Eagle memorial pole, was very, very old but in good condition except for the base, which had rotted to such an extent that the pole seemed to stand by a miracle. A light touch set it to trembling. Carved from a huge cedar log, it measured five and a half feet tall with a diameter through the widest part of more than four feet. Close by were the graves of a mother and her two sons. We cleared away the in-crowding brush and took a picture of the proud old bird, which later became one of my most successful *Alaska Sportsman* covers.

There weren't any new timing chains for Regal Diesels at the cannery in Rose Inlet to replace the one that had broken, but there was Henry Munson, a regular wizard with refractory motors. Henry was skipper of one of the cannery tenders. For three days and most of three nights he spent all his spare time working with Vady on the motor. Most of the parts they needed had to be made at the machine shop. We were forever grateful to Henry and the superintendent of the cannery for their kindness and co-operation while we were there.

Clyde insisted on waiting until we were ready to go, but Vady finally convinced him that there was no use tying up two boats just because one was broken down. We'd meet them at Hole-in-the-Wall as soon as we were fixed up.

On the fourth day we started north alone.

"We won't have any more motor trouble now," Vady said. "That Henry's a whiz. He's sure a fine mechanic. He fixed this old baby as good as new. Not only the timing chain, but he found several other little things I'd been worrying about. The coupling on the fuel pump never has been just right so he rigged up a new one. Our motor troubles are over, Babe."

"Don't brag so much about it. You're just tempting Fate again."

"Can't I even say what's true without getting into trouble with that old biddy? What does she look like, anyway?"

"Don't call her an old biddy. She won't like it. She doesn't look like anything. What does Mother Nature look like? Fate is made of the same—the same material —or whatever it is."

"I know, a scrawny old thing with big flopping ears. I know the type. Nosy, snoopy, always got her big mouth open making trouble. I don't like some of your pals."

"Go ahead, smart man, scoff and sneer. You'll laugh once too often, then you'll wish you'd listened to—"

"I'll wish I'd listened to Mamma, won't I? Babe, you're a true femme."

I'll always think I showed marvelous restraint when, a mere two hours later, the motor conked out and I didn't even peep, "I told you so." Vady looked so beaten I didn't have the heart.

On his way below he paused in the pilothouse long enough to whisper behind his hand, "Fate! She caught us! Why don't you be more careful?"

Though we were well out from shore and there were no boats in sight, I hung a towel on the mast anyway. No telling how long we would be here, and the water was getting rough again.

"The motor's hot as a firecracker," Vady said, coming back from below. "I'll have to wait until it cools before I can look it over. It sounds like a bearing. I'll take the skiff and pull the *Emblem* into that harbor. There's a dock farther in, and the wind's in the right direction to help."

We untied the skiff and tried to launch it, but each time a wave broke over and swamped it. Then it was a struggle to get it back on deck and dump it. Finally we got it in the water. Vady bailed it out and, taking the towline from the *Emblem,* got into the skiff and began to row. He pulled. He rowed harder. The *Emblem* drifted backward with the tide. He pulled and strained and grunted, his face growing redder and redder, perspiration soaking his shirt. The *Emblem* continued to drift—backward. He finally had to give up.

Now that the motor had cooled, it started reluctantly and we limped into View Cove, where there had once been a large cement-plant operation. As we came in we saw an old man, the watchman, rowing toward us in a skiff, and standing on the stern thwart was a small deer. After we had tied to the dock, the watchman invited us up to his cabin.

The deer, he explained, he had found in the woods as a fawn, evidently an orphan. He'd brought it home and raised it on condensed milk. It had the run of the house and was as tame as a kitten.

After he had made us coffee we returned to the boat, where Vady worked the rest of the afternoon on the motor and was sure it would be all right. He ran it for several hours while we were tied to the wharf and it didn't heat up. But when we went out the next morning we broke down again in exactly the same spot as the day before.

"This must be old Fate's hangout," Vady said.

"What we need is a theme song," I told him, "something like 'Drifting and Dreaming.'" I was feeling good. The sun was bright and warm, the water smooth, and far down the channel I saw the poles of a troller coming our way.

An hour later I didn't feel so gay. Vady stood on deck waving a towel as the troller came near, but she turned out in the channel and passed us by.

"Must be the brother to the fellow in McHenry Anchorage," I guessed. "The *Turquoise* of Ketchikan. I don't like people who name their boats after jewels, anyway."

It was a good hunch. We became better acquainted with the *Turquoise* later and liked her even less.

When a cannery tender came in sight several hours later, Vady put up a signal hard to ignore—a sheet, fluttering from the mast. The tender was still some distance away when she blew her whistle twice and headed toward us.

Within fifteen minutes the *Emblem,* the boat that couldn't break down, was tied beside the *Bonita* and headed for Craig. Lucky again! The *Bonita*'s destination was the very place we wanted to go.

It was a pleasant trip. Even Tlevik Narrows wasn't alarming from a vessel that seemed so able to cope with the currents. The cook prepared an excellent dinner I enjoyed immensely. For once I didn't have to ponder over which can to open. Indeed, it was the most delightful breakdown we had all summer.

At Craig we learned that Vady's guess had been right. A burned-out bearing. There was no hope of fixing up the old Diesel this time. The further he probed, the worse he found things. We'd have to go to Ketchikan by plane, then if we were lucky—or, as Vady put it, "If our good luck continues"—we might find a new motor for sale.

Our "good luck continued" on the plane, at least, for, instead of whisking us over the mountains to Ketchikan in a mere thirty minutes, we had a four-hour ride that took us over more Alaskan waters than we'd traveled all summer.

There was a passenger for a fox farm, and as we spiraled downward for the landing in a narrow spit, the treetops were so close I expected the wings of the plane to cut them off like a scythe.

Perhaps, as we passed over Coronation Island, my enjoyment of the ride would have been less had I been able to foresee the experience we were to have in these same waters. So wide, so open to the sweep of the ocean!

We couldn't talk above the noise of the plane, so we sat with our noses to the window absorbing new impressions of the country.

Far below us a fishing boat, looking no bigger than a gnat, was making its endless drags. What was the fisherman thinking in that toy boat so far beneath us? We knew, for we were fishermen too. He was hoping the hope of all of us, that this would be that hundred-dollar day he'd dreamed of all summer. The fisherman on the water and the fisherman in the sky were one in their dreams, hopes, and ambitions, for we had wings for only a few short hours.

We were seeing new aspects of the water, and for me, at least, they were not reassuring. That large brown patch of streamlined drifting leaves was kelp, growing on a dangerous reef; the shores of that beautiful little island, with its spruce topknot, seemed to go straight down. It looked at first glance as if a boat might anchor there in safety. But deep water is blue or green. It doesn't have the silvery sheen of those surrounding shoals.

And the points! No wonder Vady had warned me away from them time and again. They didn't end as points should, where the rocks disappeared beneath the surface! Brown shadows showed that they went out and out. How much lead rested on those underwater prolongations? Lead lost by fishermen intent upon cutting corners. How well I knew!

It was fun to climb the mountains in a plane. This was an amphibious plane and the pilot followed the waterways whenever he could. Sometimes it was necessary to go up and over and soar through narrow mountain passes. Too narrow, I was sure, for the spread of the wings.

I'd always wanted to see the mountaintops. Now I was seeing them without the exertion of a climb. The tops were much like the bottoms, where we had followed the game trails, except that the trees were stunted and scrubby and the growth less dense than below. And there was muskeg, even on mountaintops! And moss, bright sienna and raw umber, surrounding the brackish pools of brown water. There were lakes, too. Surprising little mountain lakes, sparkling like rare green and blue jewels in their green velvet cases.

We crossed a ridge and far below us the Pacific Ocean was shrouded in fog. We glided out into space and dropped swiftly, the descent leaving us breathless as from a ride in an express elevator.

Wisps of vapor floated by the windows. The pilot followed the shore line, so bold and rugged it made Cape Chacon seem like a bathing beach in comparison. The gulls, resenting the noisy giant, scattered screaming in all directions. Ahead was the Bay of Pillars with its spirelike columns of stone spiking the water. How frightening they would have been from the pilothouse of the *Emblem!* But we skimmed over them, struck the water in a burst of flying spray, and taxied to a stop.

Two more passengers came aboard and we flew back on what we hoped was a compass course, for it was very foggy until we crossed the mountains again. An injured man was waiting at our last stop, a wilderness logging camp, to be taken to a doctor in Ketchikan.

I was proud of my ability to pick out landmarks as we soared over Clarence Strait. There below us was McHenry Anchorage. I could see the very rocks where the *Emblem* had almost met our friend Fate. There were the islands and rocks, pinnacles and kelp beds that had been so confusing on that hot spring day—many more of them than we'd thought. But behind them was a long channel of clear water with several fishing boats in sight.

Those jumbled logs, so like a maze puzzle, were fish traps, one or two on every point. What I thought for a moment was a flock of ducks on the water was in reality five trollers bound for Ketchikan with their loads, running away from their wakes.

A bare, bald mountainside obstructed our view. "Snoose" Norwald could spit that far on a calm day! Surely the wings would scrape the rocks! But the pilot seemed unconcerned, so there must be no danger. I looked closely among the crags, hoping to see a mountain goat.

Then below us was Sunny Point, the mill, the wanigan! We were home!

Our good luck continued, for the very next day Vady found a Chrysler Ace motor for sale, hard as they were to get. He loaded it onto a tender bound for Craig and went back that same night to install it.

Five glorious days at home! Walking through our five-room mansion! Bathing night and morning in our beautiful old-fashioned bathtub! Breathing deep and full with room to spare! Sleeping at night in our marvelous springless wartime bed! I hadn't realized how tired I was from day after day of fishing and the strain of our frequent breakdowns. But I'd go back. The summer was half over and you don't give up halfway merely because your nerves jangle at the sight of an Egg Wobbler.

Then came a message from my husband, "Come at once by plane to Craig. If you aren't here tomorrow will be in to get you."

Chapter 18

Craig is a beautiful little town. I had plenty of time to look it over while Vady was finishing the installation of the new motor. The location is an island, now connected to the mainland by a dirt fill. We thought the service establishments a little out of proportion, with nine liquor stores and bars to a resident population of about two hundred. The entire island was crisscrossed by boardwalks, dividing it into city blocks with a light at each intersection. The founders must have expected a much larger growth than ever developed. Walking at night was like walking in an electrically lighted jungle, as most of the island had never been built up and brush and vines had nearly buried the sidewalks in many places.

We enjoyed the novelty of a movie and eating in a restaurant. We bought magazines and the paper from Ketchikan, the *Daily Alaska Fishing News,* and laughed together over an item we found that told graphically just what we had come to expect:

> K. Trott, of the trolling boat *Geneva,* is going back to where he "come" from; back, he says, to a country where a man can troll without snarling up in a mess of rocks every few fathoms. Up this way, he says, a man can go clear around an island and have head winds all the way. He wants no more of it, and is advertising for a couple of men to go south with him.

Oh yes, Mr. Trott, you certainly have something there, we agreed.

Here, as in Rose Inlet, the superintendent of the Libby, McNeill & Libby cannery was most helpful. He allowed us to keep the *Emblem* at the cannery wharf for the ten days it took to remove the old toad piece by piece and install the new motor. The mechanic there wanted an old Diesel for a shore pump, so he installed the new motor in exchange for the toad. We were lucky again! That took care of the installation costs—but there was still the motor itself to pay for.

The trip back to Hole-in-the-Wall was a pleasure. With our new motor we made good time without any unpleasant incidents to mar the trip.

There were at least twenty boats tied to the float the day we arrived, although it was a good fishing day. It didn't look very encouraging. There were the *Dobbs,* Flick Greer's *Taku Wind,* and the *Skookum,* with Nina and Clyde waving to us from the float.

After we had tied up and Clyde had looked over the new motor, we sat in the galley making plans.

"I don't know where to go next," Clyde said. "The weather is so bad with westerlies every afternoon that we've only been able to fish two or three days a week. When we can go out there are no fish. Flick and Dobbs are going north to Cape Pole. We don't know what to do. Nina says we have to catch some fish or else."

"Beth seems to feel the same way," Vady said, "but heck, we aren't beat by a long shot. We still have almost two months."

"I don't know," Clyde said doubtfully. "I've been thinking we might as well go in. It's just another of those off years. What's the use of burning up what we've made buying gas? As far as that goes, we haven't even made gas money since we came here."

"Then the thing to do is try somewhere else," Vady said. "Hole-in-the-Wall isn't the only place. Suppose we try Point Baker?"

"All right, but if it isn't any better than here we might as well run in. I'd like to get a job before the fleet gets in. It'll be tough finding one later on."

"If you'd get up earlier in the morning maybe we'd catch more," Nina said. "We could be out right now. There's no westerly today."

"You don't see Dobbs and Flick out, do you? No use going with them staying in."

"I don't see what that has to do with it," Nina said impatiently. "We aren't fishing with them."

"The little woman's illogical," Clyde said, then to Nina, "Because, darling, they're two of the best fishermen in the fleet, and if they can't catch them, neither can I."

With that settled we took the skiffs and went ashore to explore an interesting group of cabins. There were fifteen or twenty cabins lined up along the beach. It had once been an Indian village humming with activity, when the Indians brought in their hand-caught salmon to dry for the winter. Now the cabins were falling into ruins. Some, with foundations rotted away, lay tiredly on their sides. Some had been used recently, either by hand-trollers earlier in the season or by trappers during the winter. All had weathered to that lovely silver gray of unpainted, rain-beaten wood.

In among the islands, in remote and isolated places, we often saw deserted villages such as this. It made me feel sad, as if Alaska were a ghost country and, having reached the peak of its development, were now going backward. But around the next bend might be a little home or a mine in operation. Many times on some rocky beach or wind-swept shore we saw homes in the making. Brave little beginnings, backed up against the wilderness, fighting for a foothold. Sometimes it was a boat on the beach and a puff of smoke in the trees indicating a pioneer. Or it might be a small cabin, raw and bare, with clothes fluttering on a line and little children playing on the shore. This was new country, a growing country. All these things were only phases of its growth.

Hole-in-the-Wall is a favorite haunt of fishermen. There were many "float bums" here, men who go out to some quiet, well-protected scow, tie to the float, and sleep the summer away, fishing only when the spirit moves them or supplies run low. There were many conveniences on the scow—a washing machine for the use of the fishermen, showers, a magazine exchange, well-stocked store and restaurant.

When we went back to the float a young war veteran was entertaining a group with his stories. His boat, an eighteen-foot skiff powered with the same type of engine used on power mowers, seemed too small and cluttered for sleeping room. Early in the year he had made the long trip from Seattle in it.

In Seymour Narrows, in the inside passage, where, because of a dangerous rock in mid-channel, even good-sized boats lay to awaiting slack tide, he had run through on the flood. "Just curious," he said, "to see what those eddies and whirlpools would do to a small boat." He was going north by way of Dry Pass, a crooked passage that goes nearly dry at low tide. Of course he meant to run it at low tide, ". . . just for the fun of it."

I was glad when Vady suggested we go aboard and have supper. After all, the season wasn't over yet, and I was afraid that young man might prove a bad influence.

We had just finished supper when Sonny Dobbs came aboard.

"Hi, missus," he said. "Paw says do you want to go after abalones? The tide's awful low. We catched us a mess last night. I wouldn't eat 'em, they stink. Paw says he'll grease my tongue with a bacon rind, then I'll eat 'em, by golly."

"Sure I want to go," I said, jumping up and putting on my jacket. "I've never seen an abalone up here. Are they like the ones in California?"

"Naw, not so big," Sonny said, doubling up his fist and making a swipe at Vady's nose. "Come on, you, you'll have to take your own skiff. Ours won't hold you and the old lady."

We followed Dobbs and Sonny out to the rocks near the mouth of the harbor, where the minus tide had uncovered wonders we'd seldom seen. The rocks were covered with some pink deposit, and when we looked down into the water, silvery sea moss waved tiny fronds, looking like a forest of miniature frosted Christmas trees. Spiny pincushions, little sea urchins of lavender, rose, gray, and various shades of pink, clung to the rocks. Patches of bright green and coral growths glowed bright against brown kelp. It took a lot of hunting to find the abalones; their color and texture were so similar to the rocks on which they grew. Sometimes we would spot one with its bright orange muscle extended and the shell turning slowly on top. These were easy to get if we moved quickly and grabbed them before they clamped down on the rock. But if we fumbled, they stuck so tight they had to be pried off with a knife.

Sonny was in ecstasy, running over the slippery rocks, discovering new wonders in every crack and crevice. "Looky, missus," he yelped, holding up a brown object shaped like a Chinese slipper, "gumboot. Paw says minks eat 'em. Not me." He threw it far out onto the water as if afraid Dobbs might force it on him with the bacon rind. He stuck his hand into a crevice in the rocks, withdrew it quickly, and rubbed it on his overalls in disgust. The crevices were full of sticky, slimy starfish in every possible color—all sizes from five-pointed ones to great sunbursts with twenty rays, or legs, wedged closely together in a tangled mass awaiting the incoming tide. Our search was so interesting and successful it was dark when we returned to the float.

We reached Point Baker early in the afternoon of the next day. All along the way reports had been discouraging. No fish. It was no better at Point Baker. After some fisherman there had told us about "Ma Baker," we decided to go on. Ma was an eighty-foot whale that had been there for years. She was so friendly she came into the harbor at night, in among the boats. Although we didn't see her we weren't anxious to have her scratching her barnacles on the *Emblem*.

We had just let down our lines off Rookery Island, on

our way to Snow Pass, to try one likely-looking spot, when we looked back to see the *Skookum* dead in the water. What a boost to the *Emblem*'s morale! She swished her skirts in a smart turn and in a few moments we were gliding through the water with the *Skookum* in tow, the *Emblem* proud that for once she was furnishing the power.

Wrangell was the nearest town where repairs might be made, we couldn't make the long distance before dark, so after all we got to spend a night in Quiet Harbor!

Nina and I enjoyed the stay in Wrangell while the men put a new drive shaft in the *Skookum.* Eating in restaurants was a treat to Clyde and Nina. We went to a movie and had baths at the hotel. True, it rained most of the time, but one afternoon the sun came out, so Nina and I took our sketch pads and covered the town.

Some Indian children, seeing us at work, came over to watch us, standing close and joggling our elbows in their efforts to see. When we were ready to go, Nina asked them all down to the drugstore for ice-cream cones while I went back to the boat to start supper.

While we were there, a packer came in with a report of a big coho run at Cape Pole. The men worked nearly all night to finish the work on the *Skookum,* and we left after they had snatched a few hours' sleep.

There was a heavy fog. Steering by compass was nothing new to me now. Vady had often complimented me on my navigating, saying I could read a chart better than most of the fishermen. What he didn't know was that I considered it a matter of life and death. I wanted to *know* where we were, and to know I had to watch the chart closely. Feeling so sure of myself, I got a severe jolt when the fog lifted an hour later to reveal Woronkofski

Island dead ahead. According to my calculations, we should have been at least a mile offshore.

Vady took a bearing and set a new course for the Eye-Opener light, telling me to be a little more careful. This time, I vowed, I wouldn't let the compass swing a fraction of a degree. That jittery lubber line wasn't going to outwit me a second time.

Three hours later the sun came out to stay, and there was the Eye-Opener twenty degrees to starboard! Thoroughly discouraged, I turned over the problems of navigation to the mate. After a little experimenting he solved the difficulty. The new motor had changed the deviation of the compass. Removing one of the compensating magnets was all that was needed to correct it.

At Cape Pole we went into Fisherman's Harbor with the aid of a light onshore that we lined up with a light on a rock in the entrance. There were two scows in the harbor, one buying for a Wrangell concern, the other for a Ketchikan company.

"The run only lasted two days," the buyer from Ketchikan, "Lefty" Hogan, told us. "It was a ding dandy while it lasted! One of the fishermen made four hundred dollars two days hand-running."

"Isn't that the way?" Clyde said with a shrug. "Hear about a run and it's over when you get there."

"How are the boats doing now?" Vady asked.

"About twenty or thirty dollars a day. Flick made fifty yesterday. His was the highest boat."

"That's not too bad," Vady said. "If we could average twenty or thirty a day, with a chance of getting in on another run, we'd make out."

"I've a notion to run in," Clyde said. "It doesn't look good to me."

"Oh, Clyde, let's stay," Nina begged. "If other boats can make three hundred a day, we can too."

"The little lady evidently expects a run," Clyde laughed. "What do I care? I'd only have to hunt a job anyway."

"Do you fellows belong to the union?" Lefty asked. "Flick Greer has been stirring up trouble among the fishermen. It's a mess."

"As far as I know we belong," Vady told him. "We joined before we came out, but a man hardly knows how he stands. When they organized, why didn't they spend a little more time on it and get their contracts drawn up so they would know and the fishermen would know what's what?"

We found out just how muddled things were before many days had passed. In fact, with one thing and another Cape Pole turned out to be the most exciting place we fished.

Chapter 19

Back in the days before statehood Uncle Sam made it easy for his people to own land in Alaska. Upon request the Forest Service would survey a five-acre tract for a homesite. One paid a small yearly fee, built a habitable dwelling, lived on the land for three years, and could then prove up on it. Or a use permit might be obtained for those who did not care to own the land. In that case the exclusive use of the land was theirs as long as they paid a small annual fee. When they no longer wanted the land, it reverted to the public domain.

At Fisherman's Harbor, Cape Pole, there were about a dozen homesites thus acquired. The year-rounders were three families and several bachelors. Some of the homes were built of beachcombed lumber; some had been floated in from other locations. There were several from Edna Bay, where a number of small buildings had been left vacant when the wartime Alaska Spruce Program was completed.

The Tylers, year-rounders who had charge of the Wrangell scow, had three children. Another family had a son, Bobby. Bobby came aboard the *Emblem* one night and had supper with us. When I asked him what the children did about school, he said there was a correspondence course available from Juneau and that his father, a former college professor, helped the children with their studies.

Fishing was the livelihood of these settlers, augmented during the winter months by trapping and hand-logging. During the winter things were quiet around Cape Pole. The mail boat, stopping once a month, furnished their only contact with the busy outside world.

"Pikepole Slim" and his wife had reached the goal Vady had in mind when he bought the *Emblem*—the enviable state of living off the land, that dream that lures so many to Alaska. What matter to them if pork chops were forty cents each in Ketchikan? None, while Slim had the eye of an eagle and a trigger finger like greased lightning.

All surplus food garnered through the season was canned. Slim's cellar resembled a well-stocked delicatessen. Blueberries and salmonberries, red huckleberries and wild strawberries were canned or made into jam. There were jars of oysters and clams, crab, shrimp, and octopus—this last, by the way, we sampled and found good, with a flavor much like crab. There were canned wild rhubarb and asparagus in Slim's cellar, goose tongue and beach grass, canned duck and goose. Over in the corner was a keg of salt salmon. Fresh fish could be caught at any time, and bear meat, goat, and venison were added to their larder in season.

In a small garden beside the house the cabbages grew as big as deck buckets, and fat carrots pushed their orange heads impatiently above the soil. Parsnips and potatoes, beets, lettuce, and kale for the chickens filled every available space. Against a fence red raspberries were just coming into bearing and there was a little strawberry bed beside the chicken coop.

The inside of the house was likewise distinctive, for Slim, graduate of a correspondence course in taxidermy, had a wild-game frieze around the wall—a deer head, squirrel, duck, and goose, all of his own mounting.

After this revealing glimpse into the art of living off the land I had a better understanding of Vady's dream.

With merely the addition of a pot-bellied stove and a cracker barrel, the general store in Fisherman's Harbor, owned by a retired sea captain, would have made a perfect setting for a Hollywood production. We entered through a lean-to that served as the hardware department. It contained a most amazing conglomeration of new and used motor parts, stove parts, fishing gear, tools, shovels, traps, chains—anything and everything, it seemed, that could possibly be used by hunter and trapper, fisherman or logger.

The grocery department in the main part of the building was equally complete. The first thing we noticed was a coin box on a window sill, stacked full of silver coins so black and tarnished that only their size showed their value. Perhaps they were left there as evidence of the old captain's financial standing, for he made change from a drawer under the counter. Besides groceries he had a good stock of overalls, underwear, and canvas gloves.

The earthquake-born tidal wave of several months earlier, which destroyed the Scotch Cap Light Station on Unimak Pass, with a loss of five lives, and swept with devastating force upon parts of the Hawaiian Islands, had reached Fisherman's Harbor, diminished in size but still destructive. All day, the residents said, the water surged in and out of the harbor, smashing small boats, washing out bulkheads, tearing floats from their moorings and beaching them far up in the lagoon, then receding to leave the lagoon dry.

To those who yearn for peaceful isolation Fisherman's Harbor may sound ideal. But even this apparent Utopia was not free from the pettiness and jealousy that plague the world. Once they had a duel, Pikepole Slim told us, that disturbed the tranquillity of the entire settlement.

All spring there had been keen rivalry between "Hangover" Johnson and John Ridges as to which of them would have the larger halibut catch at the end of the season. Hangover was a crotchety old codger in his late sixties, tall, lean, and angular, while John was just the opposite—a little dumpling of a man with pink cheeks and white hair, and the happy disposition that often seems to go with excessive fat. They were inseparable cronies.

Small bets among the settlers became larger bets as the season advanced. The two factions were about evenly divided, however. John and Hangover had both made friends, but for different reasons—the one for his unfailing good humor and fund of stories, the other for his keg of home-brew generously shared.

Excitement ran high as first one was in the lead and then the other. Late afternoon would find the settlers straggling toward the beach, waiting for the boats to come in. All during the season John's and Hangover's catches remained about even.

Then one evening John came in with a record load when Hangover had been all but skunked. Hangover was furious, and the good-natured gibes of the John faction did nothing to ease his temper. He stalked away to his cabin and poured out a big slug of brew, but even that didn't help. At last he could stand it no longer. He grabbed his gun from the wall and with hate in his heart and fire in his eyes walked around the beach to John's cabin.

"Come out of that dump, you polecat," he snarled. "I've took all I'm goin' to offen you! We'll settle this matter here and now!"

John, puzzled by his friend's anger, came to the door.

"You get first chance," Hangover said, thrusting the gun into John's hand. "I'll walk to that tree yonder and you shoot. If you miss me, it's my turn. You walk to the tree and I get to shoot at you."

Pretending to agree, John took the gun. He stood waiting, with the gun on his shoulder, as Hangover began his death march. Then with a mighty heave he hurled the gun out into the lagoon.

"Now come back here, you crazy ape," he bellowed, "and keep on a-movin'. Don't you never set foot on my place again, nor let me hear no more of your damned-fool talk!"

It was at Cape Pole that we met Carl Henning, one of our most interesting contacts of the entire summer. Years ago Carl had had the misfortune to lose his left arm, but he still fished his four-poled troller, alone and unassisted, although well over sixty years of age. Like many other old-timers he still preferred the carefree life of an outdoor man to living in town. During trapping season he would go out by himself and, anchored in some little cove, run a trap line on the beach.

Carl owned his own home in Ketchikan, so he didn't face the possibility of one old-timer Vady talked to. This old fellow was in his eightieth year. "When are you going to give up fishing and settle down?" Vady asked him.

"Never," the old fellow answered. "Not while I still have the strength to sock a salmon over the head and the money for a box of snoose. Soon's I quit fishin' they'll grab me and stick me in the old men's home in Sitka. I ain't an old man yet, by a long shot."

By the same token Carl wasn't an old man by a long shot either. He made up his own gear, cleaned his fish, pulled his anchor, shot his yearly allowance of two deer, and did his own cooking. One night on the scow some men were attempting to set a wolf trap. It was a big, ugly brute of a thing with two strong springs.

"Here," Carl said, "let me show you." With his one hand and a nail to hold one of the springs while he pushed down the other, he set the trap with ease. To me Carl seemed to prove that modern living hasn't softened all men into helpless sissies. Cheerful, helpful, and optimistic, he entertained us many times with tales of his Alaskan adventures.

We thought we detected a trace of apology in his voice when he told us, "Two hundred fish a day are about all I can handle any more. It takes me so long to clean 'em." Two hundred fish! Ye gods! We'd heard young men groan at the thought of cleaning half that many!

Carl had solved the problem of one-handed cleaning very ingeniously. Hooking the fish head over a nail in the cockpit, he'd hold it steady with the stump of his left arm while he wielded the knife with his good right hand.

Many strange and amusing tales are told on the fishermen. Old "Dirty-Face" O'Brian, *Stinky*'s original owner, was responsible for his share. One night he ran out of gas just outside the harbor. His fishing partner towed him in and was surprised when Dirty-Face insisted upon being towed to a tug anchored there instead of to the scow where there was gas for sale. The mystery was solved in the summer moonlight. There was Dirty-Face on the stern of the tug, siphoning gas from a drum on deck into his own tank. For a hose he was using, of all things, the long, hollow whip from a piece of giant kelp.

There was the man who bought a nine-dollar roll of nylon leader. He was mucking out his boat and he laid the roll on deck. While he was scrubbing down the deck a group of fishermen came by. In the excitement of the ensuing conversation he picked up the roll of leader and hurled it overboard. Furious at his own stupidity, he went into the scow and bought another. Five minutes later he repeated the costly performance.

One cheechako, fishing his first day, had the good fortune to run into cohos. The fish came so fast he left all the cleaning until he came in at night. At two in the morning he was still at it, so tired and groggy his movements were almost mechanical. Suddenly he came to with a start. There on the deck, carefully laid out in a neat row, were the viscera of his fish. He had thrown the fish overboard. That story reminded us of Clyde's sleepwalking escapade.

It happened at Kaigani. We'd had a particularly busy day during one of the coho runs. Clyde hadn't been sleeping well anyway and he was dog tired that night. He pulled off his clothes and crawled into his bunk naked. About daylight Nina woke up. Clyde's bunk was empty. She jumped up and ran to the pilothouse. There stood Clyde, a tall white taper in the dim light, grasping the wheel and peering feverishly through the window.

"Clyde!" Nina gasped. "What in the world are you doing? We're tied to the trap. Come back to bed."

"Don't tell me what I'm doing!" Clyde shouted, putting the wheel hard over. "I'm trying to miss that boat!"

But a fisherman can't sit around and yarn all day.

At Cape Pole we had nineteen days of straight sunshine, a good record for Southeastern Alaska. But weather is just one of the details that prevent a fisherman's life from becoming monotonous. Imagine you are with us for a typical day of fishing the *Emblem.*

We get an early start and the sun is just striking the highest peaks as Vady starts the motor. We'll have breakfast later on. Now that we've made the break, getting out of the warm bunk into the chill of the galley, we hate to lose any time. The fish may be hitting on the incoming tide.

The mountains here are bold and rugged, their bare cliffs glowing pink with the rising sun. They stand out like pastel etchings against the blue of the sky. We wish again that some more aesthetic soul had named the Nipples, those two majestic peaks to our left!

Out of Fisherman's Harbor we run slowly, steering carefully among the beds of growing kelp. A row in the skiff has revealed the jagged rocks lying just beneath the surface of the water where the roots of the kelp have their tenacious hold. Well past the kelp we speed up to "throw a charge into the batteries" as we head out into deep water. We slow to trolling speed, Vady is putting out the lines.

There is no wind this morning, and we are thankful, but the water is still rough from yesterday's westerly. The winds blow in from the ocean every afternoon, as regular as the tides though much more upsetting.

Already Vady has begun to yell. By the end of the day

I'll be convinced he is angry with me. Otherwise why would he make those awful faces? He'll tell me his throat is raw from shouting, and I'll think of Nina's remark: "Clyde wouldn't be able to fish with anyone but me. No one else on earth would stand being yelled at like that, day after day."

There it is again!

"What?" sticking my head out the door.

"Power!" he screeches. "Give me the POWER!"

After a quick look around to see that all is clear, I stand in the door. I must be ready for further instructions.

Another pole is wobbling.

"When you get that one in," I scream in turn, "take the one on the other side!"

With two fish in the boat before he even had the lines all out, we think this may possibly turn out to be a record day.

Which way shall we go? Most of the boats are fishing to the south, off the cape. But we had good luck yesterday at Point Hardscrabble, two and a half miles north of the cape. It's not an easy place to fish—the chart shows deep water to the kelp line, but we've hit bottom more than once with fifteen fathoms of line out. I'd better check with the fisherman.

"How many fathoms today?"

"Ten."

I wonder. More than once he's told me that, and I've later learned, to my chagrin and our expense, that he's had out fifteen or twenty fathoms. It's a little hoax of his to get me in closer to shore. I don't think it's very cute; a pilot has trouble enough without being mizzled about the depths. To counteract it, I am forced to lie about the depths marked on the chart, swearing that we're in *very* shallow water. This often leads to an impasse all around.

Experience has taught us to stay well away from the rocks until we are safely around Hardscrabble. One day, goaded by his insistence that I get closer to the rocks, I made a short cut and found us in water breaking white on a shoal. I made a quick outturn—not quick enough to save our gear.

Around the point we can swing in and follow the kelp line quite close to the shore. There's a deep hole here where the feed collects, and usually we find cohos.

The tide has changed and is coming in fast. Swirls and eddies make little waves that lap against the sides of the boat. The drifting kelp is gathering into twisted masses. When traveling so slowly the boat responds sluggishly to the wheel, and I'm kept busy dodging kelp and logs and trying to keep on course.

This is a good morning! Vady is busy as a beaver. He has all he can do to keep the lines in the water as he pulls first one and then another. The fish are deep. More often than not they take the bottom spoon. That means he has to unsnap six leaders from the line, snap them onto the wire across the stern where they dangle in the water while he lands the fish, unsnap them from the wire, and snap them onto the line again as he lets it out. It all takes time when time is valuable.

He's calling. I go to the door.

"Look, Beth! I caught one on the leader. It took the spoon while it was still dangling from the stern, just as I was reaching for it."

We meet the *Skookum*. Our poles almost touch as we come close to compare our luck.

"Two cohos and a fifteen-pound red!" Clyde yells.

"Fourteen cohos," Vady reports.

Oh! Oh! Vady will be asking for inside turns when the cohos slack off. We'll be scraping the rocks all afternoon!

Offshore I see a flock of gulls fluttering over the water, screaming and diving as they feed on a school of herring. We'll circle the feed as close as we can without frightening the birds. If the gulls fly the herring will shatter the surface of the water with a mass leap and disappear into the depths. The salmon will follow them. We are a scant boat length away when the gulls fly.

A rubbery black back appears where the birds were feeding! Two baleful eyes look straight into mine. A yawning cavern opens up, spewing herring to right and left! At close range I am gazing at the tonsils of a whale!

My stomach folds into a tight wad as he arches his back out of the water and rolls under again, leaving an oily slick.

"A whale!" I scream. "Did you see that?"

"Sure, what of it? Ignore him and he'll go away," Vady laughs. Laughs, mind you!

I lose all interest in gulls, herring, and salmon. Only one thing matters now—to put as much water between us and that whale as possible before he comes to the surface again. I don't dare speed up the motor, although I'm tempted to. The fisherman would be furious! Making a wild guess that the whale will continue to feed along the rip, I head in the other direction, toward shore.

Three whales have been around Cape Pole ever since we came, but they've never been so close as today. Often they lie out in the channel, their backs barely showing. Sometimes they put on a gigantic show, jumping clear out of the water or slapping their great flukes on the surface with a tremendous splash that sends geysers of water high in the air. Fishermen tell us they act this way during mating season, which doesn't add anything to my peace of mind.

To stay away from where I think the whale is, I must

keep inside the rip. That is where all the drift is collecting. If I can get between that log and the kelp beds, we'll be in the clear again and I can swing out.

It's happened! Vady's voice. "Let's make an inside turn. We might pick up a king."

Darn and double darn! Of all the times for him to think of inside turns, it had to be now! I'll argue with him! But when I step outside he's busy with a fish and doesn't hear me.

I should never have left the wheel! We're right on top of a drifting kelp bed. With the tide pushing against the bow I can't turn the damned old boat. Nothing to do but plow through and hope we save our gear!

"Kelp!" I yell. "We're in it!"

Vady grabs a tag line to ease the strain on the creaking pole. The kelp runs down the lines and collects in masses at the angle of the tag lines. All the poles bend back with the weight of the tangled kelp. We hear the propeller grinding it to bits. A tag line breaks, and then another!

In the clear at last, Vady reels in the lines. One broken, the lead gone from another, all the leaders tangled together in a hopeless mess. It's going to take him a long time to straighten them out, but still we're lucky. The propeller didn't foul. He's too much of a diplomat to blame me outright, but I don't like his implication when he asks, "Were you taking a little snooze?" This is the ideal time to go below and make breakfast.

It's nearly ten o'clock. No wonder we're starved, but no fisherman would stop to eat when the fish are hitting. I prepare bacon and eggs and warm up some butterhorns we bought in Wrangell. There's a little green mold along the edges, but I scrape that off. Penicillin is made from mold, we understand, so it's probably good for us. Mold has become very common in our lives, with the inside of the boat damp at all times. The bread isn't fresh when it reaches the scow, and it might be a week or ten days between trips. We've learned to disregard mold, unless a loaf gets to looking like Roquefort cheese. A few moments in the oven freshen it up.

After my breakfast the fish stop biting. The two large whales have kept me uneasy all morning, spouting first on one side of the boat and then the other. I keep wondering when they'll come up under the boat. I haven't chased any more gulls. Vady goes to the galley for his breakfast.

When he comes up he looks around. "Where in heck are we?" he asks. "How did we get into all this kelp?"

I look around and then I see we are in a veritable garden of kelp. It's growing everywhere. Large beds and small beds, with very narrow zigzag trails of clear water between. How did we get here? I don't know. I was watching the whales.

"Watch what you're doing now. I'll take in the lines."

I slide between two beds. There's barely room for the *Emblem* to squeeze through. With the lines in, Vady rushes up onto the bow. I can almost read his mind, and McHenry Anchorage looms large in retrospect.

"Keep watching me now. I'll give you a signal if I see rocks ahead."

He's agitated. Or is he always so pale?

We work our way through. No harm done, but I still can't see how we got in there.

The water is calm in the lee of Warren Island, so we cross over, catching halibut after halibut on the way. The halibut season is closed, so we have to throw them back. There goes six dollars, eight, five, swimming away.

It says in the log that the stovepipe was "deep-sixed," a harmless-sounding expression. Vady decided to clean it. I saw it slip from his hands and sink. If they don't have stovepipes for sale on the scow, we're in a fix.

I go below to clean up the galley. All at once there is a terrific clatter out back. It sounds like the propeller tearing loose. I rush out on deck to find we are in the middle of another kelp patch.

"Have a nice nap?" I ask my husband. For once he has no answer. I feel no shame whatever when he later chides me for having no sympathy for his "bad luck."

"No use trolling," he says. "They aren't biting now. I'm going to try stripping. Dobbs gave me a few fresh herring this morning. Don't you want to come out in this nice warm sunshine and watch, Dolly?"

How come this sweet talk all at once?

"If you want to, you might untangle those leaders while you aren't doing anything," he says, answering my unspoken question.

He drops the anchor, gets out his rod and the herring. With a razor blade he carefully cuts a strip from each side of the herring, making a little pennant. He throws the backbones overboard. Then he goes to a lot of trouble getting the pennants on the hook just right, trying them out in the water for action, turning them a trifle, this way or that. At last he's satisfied and makes a cast. The line sinks to the bottom and he strips it in.

We've been here an hour and no fish, but he's patient. I've untangled the leaders, not minding it at all, being in such a happy mood over his encounter with the kelp.

He's caught a fish, and it's a big one! There's great excitement in landing a salmon on a rod, but he does it, and I'm proud of him.

He opens it up, and it's a red. Color is the first thing he looks for when he cleans a fish. The small difference between a white king and a red makes quite a difference in our fish slip. The second thing he looks for is what the fish are feeding on. This fish is full to the point of greediness, and, of all things, with those very backbones of the herring he had discarded.

He lost our last large lead when he hit the kelp. Not that he mentioned it. No, indeed! I learn it now, when he says we might as well go in.

The seas have built up into choppy waves. I'm anxious to get into the harbor, but Vady has put out two lines for the return trip and now I'm having trouble getting him to take them in.

At quitting time he always reminds me of the children when I used to tell them to pick up their toys and go to bed. Anything to keep the lines in the water a few minutes longer. There's always a chance of picking up one more fish. Each leader is coiled with exacting care and carefully stowed away. Each spoon is minutely examined and lovingly tucked into the spoon bucket. Leads are placed in their holders and shifted into various positions. Any little tinkering jobs that come up during the day are thankfully saved for this time. Anything to delay raising the poles so we can speed up.

We are already in the mouth of the harbor and he still has the poles to put up and secure. Since we installed the new motor I have no confidence in my ability to make a landing.

Spurt into the harbor! Throw her in reverse! Glide up to the scow and shut off the motor. That's the way Vady does it. But that glide eludes me every time.

"Hurry," I say, "we're nearly there! I want you to take the wheel."

"You can land her all right," he assures me with a grin. "Slide right in back of the scow. We'll tie there tonight."

We're coming in too fast. Even an idiot could see that.

I put her in reverse, but we continue to charge ahead. I speed up the motor, and Vady yells, "Hey, what are you trying to do? Burn out a bearing? Shut her down! Shut her down!"

I have no time for idle chitchat. He's waving his arms, motioning for me to back up. We're going to hit the scow!

We do! With a resounding bang that almost throws me off my feet, and brings Lefty running out of the scow. I move the shift and find it was in neutral instead of reverse.

Vady is examining the bow iron. He points for Lefty to look, then he glares at me, raising his shoulders in a shrug, and sighs a big sigh as much as to say, "That does it!"

A watermelon rises in my throat. Sniffing, I go below. Who asked to go fishing in the first place? Who wanted to land the damned boat? Of all the cockeyed, crazy schemes he's ever had, this one of living off the land is the worst! I'm sick to death of fish, of whales, yes, and of him! Has love flown out the porthole? This is one night I'll miss the fun of seeing our fish weighed in. On second thought, who wants to, anyway? Disgraced and downhearted, I begin peeling potatoes for supper.

Loud voices come from the scow. I forget I'm pouting and hurry on deck.

Chapter 20

I went around to the fishhouse to see what the noise was about. The *Taku Wind* had been tied to the scow when we came in. Now Johnny had come in and tied up beside her, and was scrambling across her deck with two limp, bedraggled cohos. Flick came toward him, a wrench in his hand.

"Where do you think you're going?" Flick yelled as Johnny stepped onto the scow.

"To sell my fish," Johnny said mildly.

"Oh no, you're not," Flick said, "there's going to be an end to this, you scabs unloading ahead of us union guys. I ain't unloaded yet, and you'll wait till I do." Then, turning to Lefty, who stood in the doorway, "You take his fish first and we'll close up your scow for you."

Lefty was a man of about forty-five, with shoulders and arms as muscular as a Kodiak bear. One expected him to be tough, but he was mild-mannered and courteous. With his build he could afford to be.

"You weren't ready to unload," he said reasonably. "You've been working on your motor for an hour."

"I'll decide when I'll unload," Flick snapped. "There's no scab ahead of me, understand?

"I'm a union man," he said, turning to Johnny, "and you better be one too, damned quick, if you know what's good for you."

"I'd druther be one," Johnny said, "but them fellows said a businessman didn't need to b'long."

"Any fisherman who doesn't is a scab," Flick said. "That makes you a scab."

"Fellow told me when I bought *My Chance* that I was a small businessman," Johnny said, looking scared. "Fellow said I was independent. Said businessmen had associations and organizations, no unions. I'd druther be a businessman than a scab."

"Whatever he told you, I'm telling you now. You better join up. Us union guys run things on the grounds," Flick said, his eyes flashing.

Johnny tossed his fish on the scale, but Flick jumped to the scow and with one swift movement dumped them on the floor and kicked them into a corner.

"What are you trying to pull?" he shouted. "You'll wait until I unload." He advanced threateningly toward Johnny, who backed off and cowered against the wall.

"Maybe you'd better go back to the boat," Vady whispered. I shook my head. Miss all this excitement?

"See here," Lefty said, "there's no use getting tough, Flick. This fellow has only two fish."

"Two fish, two hundred fish. What's the odds? It's the principle of the thing. Our contract says union boats first, and by God, that's the way it's going to be. You better fall in line, Lefty, you can't buy his fish anyway."

"Why not?"

"Because it says so in the contract and I'm here to see that you don't."

"Not that I've ever noticed," Lefty said. "See here," walking over to where a copy of the contract was tacked to the wall. "It says that 'in the event that the members of the union shall fail to furnish the company with all the fish his business may require, the company shall be free to purchase such fish from other available sources.' I haven't received any orders not to buy all the fish I can get. I know there's a clause that we have to unload union boats first, but why be so ornery about it?"

"That's what I said," Flick hedged, "you buy from me first."

"How can you call a man a scab just because he doesn't belong to the union? Isn't that what we fought the war for? To keep this country free?"

"Maybe you fought the war, but I'm no fool. I'm not fighting any war, past, present, or future. There's ways of getting out of that malarkey."

"Smart man," said Lefty with a short laugh. "But anyway, there's no troller's strike now."

"There damn' well will be if you buy from scabs ahead of us union men," Flick growled. "I'll meet the boats and tell 'em not to sell to you."

"You won't have to," Lefty said, "I'll tell 'em myself. I'm not against your union or any other union that's properly run, but I won't be pushed around by a lot of radicals. If the majority wants it, I'll close up the scow and you can ice to town."

The boats were coming in, idling their motors while they waited to get to the scow. The *Dobbs* slid in beside Johnny's boat, and Dobbs fastened his lines across it to the *Taku Wind*. He slouched into the fishhouse.

"What's the delay?" he asked. "Let's get on the ball. I want to unload."

"There's a little argument going on," Vady said.

"Lefty thought he'd unload this scab's fish ahead of mine," Flick put in, pointing a scornful finger at Johnny, who had picked up his fish again and now stood holding them uncertainly.

"That's why we have a contract," Flick continued. "Isn't it, Vady? You're a union man."

"Don't you get into this," I whispered nervously.

"You've got a contract, all right," Lefty said to Flick, "but I don't think it will hold water. I'll bet this union falls to pieces just the way they all have in the last twenty years. It's just like Johnny says, you own your own boats; you're in business for yourselves."

"I'll tell you what I'll do," Flick said, taking everyone into his confidence. "Lefty says he'll close the scow. My boat'll pack six thousand. I'll take the fish to town. If I can't handle 'em the larger boats could help."

"How much would you charge?" Dobbs asked.

"Six cents a pound. I figure it'd cost me four to take my fish in, what with ice and gas and the fishing time I'd lose. So six should be about right."

"Six cents!" bawled Dobbs. "Well, I'll be damned! We're payin' three now with the scow and packer, and you want six!"

"I ain't doin' it for nothing," Flick said sharply. "I ain't no charitable organization."

"You'll never get no fish outa me," Dobbs said. "Come on, Lefty, let's get goin'." Then to Flick, "You goin' to unload or not?"

All at once the fight seemed to have gone out of Flick. "I've got to get my carburator back on before dark. I'll pull up away from the door."

"Can I sell my fish now?" Johnny asked.

"Sure, throw them on," Lefty said.

As the *Taku Wind* moved away, the *Dobbs* tied up and Dobbs began pewing out his fish. Lefty picked one up, examining it critically.

"See here, Dobbs," he said, "I can't take these fish."

"Can't take 'em? Why the hell not?"

"These are creek fish. Spawners."

"They ain't neither, by God," bellowed Dobbs.

"You can't fool me on fish, Dobbs. Look at this thing!" Lefty held one aloft. "Black as tar and soft as a rag. They're not fit for food. Besides, they aren't troll-caught."

"They may have been in fresh water," Dobbs admitted, "but I caught 'em trolling off the mouth of the creek. I was out a good ways, too."

"How do you account for this?" Lefty asked, pointing to faint marks along the sides of the fish. "This is seine-caught. You can't catch a fish with a hook and gaff it without leaving a scratch anywhere."

Dobbs's face reddened. "I'll sell 'em, by damn!" he shouted. "If you won't take 'em the cannery will."

He reloaded his fish and backed away from the scow, muttering curses. As he turned toward the channel, Sonny came out on deck. His thin treble voice carried back over the water. "Paw," he piped, "this here seine's dribblin' all over the galley floor. Maw says get it out on deck or we don't get no supper."

"What's the matter with everyone all at once?" I asked

Vady as we went back to the *Emblem.* "I always thought Flick seemed nice enough. He's always upholding law and order. Of course I knew Dobbs is crooked."

"You're not a very good judge of human nature, Betsy. Everything Flick upholds is to his benefit. Like hauling the fish for six cents a pound. He saw a chance to make some money and made his offer. I used to like him but when he bragged that he made that green boy he had out last summer pay for the gear he lost, that cooled me."

"Did he really?"

"Yes. While Flick took a nap the kid hung up the gear and lost a line. He didn't know the water shallowed up there. It wasn't fair to make him pay."

In view of the fact that Flick had seemed in such a hurry to leave the scow, we were surprised a few minutes later to hear him calling Vady from our deck.

"Can you spare a few minutes?" he asked as he came down into the galley. "I've got a proposition. How would you like to make some money?"

"That's what I'm trying to do every day," Vady said, grinning. "What's on your mind?"

"Traps. Fish traps. I've got a good setup, but I need another boat. Yours will pack about eight thousand won't she?"

"A little better than that."

"I made a deal with the guy on the *Turquoise,* but he didn't show up. I had to dump three thousand. They spoiled on me while I was waiting. I worked last year on a fish trap. Naturally I wasn't doing it for my health. I made friends. The watchman on North trap is working with me, brails my boat full at night. You've probably noticed the trap patrol boat ties in here every night. Old Sidney, the guy on the patrol boat, has made himself a good thing of it. Four of us split up. Sid, the trap watchman, the fellow that owns the *Turquoise,* but he's out now, and me. Sid gets a night's sleep as a bonus and he's so old he appreciates that. If the fish come in slow so we don't get away before morning, he runs up the line and lets us know if the tenders are coming."

"No thanks, Flick. I don't want any part of trap-pirating. We can make an honest go of it."

"It ain't dishonest," Flick said. "We're paying Sid and the watchman a dollar a fish. We gaff the cohos, tear up the mouths, clean 'em and sell 'em to the scow. There's no danger of getting caught if you use your head."

"The watchman and Sid are hired by the cannery, aren't they? The trap belongs to the cannery too."

"Sure," Flick admitted easily, "but those canneries never miss a few thousand fish. One of the foremen told me if I robbed their traps, the least I could do was sell the fish to them. Anyway, the owners are rich bastards from the States. Why should they get fish that belong by rights to us fishermen here in Alaska?"

"I don't see it that way," Vady said. "Perhaps the fish traps are bad for the country, but they're licensed by law, doing legitimate business. Pirating is a dirty game."

"We all have to look after ourselves. You've had hard luck this summer and could use a little easy money. You won't take any risk," Flick insisted. "I'll pay you four cents a pound to run the humpies to the cannery and they'll never know where they came from. You'll make more money than you have all summer. Think it over, Vady, while I gas up."

"I don't have to think it over, Flick. Count me out."

"Haven't any use for the long green, I suppose," Flick said sarcastically, rubbing his fingers together. "You'll reconsider. I think the *Turquoise* is working South trap, the double-crosser, walking out on me. Old Fourpole may take a pot shot at him. He's had South trap tied up for years."

Several times after that we saw the *Turquoise,* either tied to South trap in the early-morning hours, or at dusk when we came in, laying to or moving slowly up and down the channel, waiting for dark.

This new aspect was thrilling. I felt as if we were living in the days of the buccaneers.

Chapter 21

Vady and I were having a game of double solitaire later in the evening when Nina and Clyde came over.

"Great doings on the scow tonight, I understand," Clyde said. "We didn't get in in time for the fun. When we came over, Flick was putting a union card on Johnny's boat, and what's more, he gave Johnny the twenty dollars to pay for it. Told him he could pay it back out of his fish money. Johnny won't catch twenty dollars' worth of fish before the end of the season!"

"It's the same old fight," Vady said. "It's been going on up here for twenty years. They had a union then, but someone ran off with the funds. The co-ops are a better deal. Seem to work out fine for the fishermen."

"What they should do," Clyde said, "is get that organizer to sign up the fish. They're about all that's left without a contract."

"Are you joking?" Nina asked. "How could they?"

"Of course I'm not joking," Clyde said, winking at Vady. "See, Beth, my little lady takes an interest in current events." Taking Nina's hand, he looked pleadingly into her eyes and begged, "Tell them, sweetheart, about the time I fell overboard. I shouted at you to kill the engine, remember? And what did she do but grab the hammer and beat everything off of it."

"Clyde, you liar! I did not!"

"Of course you didn't, darling," he said contritely. "I remember now. It was a wrench."

He jumped up, dragging her with him. "Let's go back to the boat," he said. "I'm hungry. Good-by, dear!" He grabbed her in his arms and kissed her.

Nina pulled away, looking ruffled. "See what I mean?" she said. "I can't understand him. He does such queer things." She sank back on the seat and was soon lost in a dream.

"Wonder where Flick got that big load yesterday," Clyde said. "He sure hit a bonanza."

"Trap-robbing," I said.

"No! Really?"

"He propositioned me tonight," Vady said, "wants me to sell the fish back to the canneries he steals them from. Pirates are thick as flies around here. Wouldn't wonder if Dobbs is in on it too."

"No, I don't think so. Dobbs is creek-robbing. We saw him today with his seine set in the mouth of Essowah Creek. He and Sonny were up to their hips in the water, driving the fish down. It's a queer thing. I don't get it. They talk about pirating as openly as if it was a recognized business. I've heard them in town bragging about how much they made at it. We saw the *Turquoise* leaving South trap this morning with her guards almost under water. I don't want any of it."

"When I was running the boats at McNeil, there were a lot of fellows there who wished they hadn't bragged," Vady laughed. "Down there in the clink, they were classed with the Eskimo who ate his wife. The Eskimo was justified in his own eyes too. He was hungry, his wife was nice and fat, and besides, he had a younger wife."

"You could almost call that cannibalism," Nina said, coming out of her reverie.

Clyde smacked his forehead with his hand. "Ladies and gentleman," he cried, jumping to his feet and lifting his arms in an expansive gesture, "you have just met my wife, who has the most remarkable insight into human nature ever seen . . ."

"Oh, Clyde, keep quiet."

"May I have your autograph, madame?" he begged. "Tell us more." He rubbed his stomach. "I don't know what's the matter with me," he complained. "Hungry, hungry, hungry all the time. We just got up from the table—at nine this morning—and I'm hungry again already."

"You must be," I said. "It's almost ten. Do you mean you haven't eaten since?"

"Not a bite. The soup kitchen was closed today. The little lady was writing an adventure story about the Swiss Alps. She's never been there, so it was heavy going. Who am I to curb budding genius at work? What was it, dear, a bicycle trip in the snow?"

"I was writing letters and you know it," Nina said indignantly. "You make me sound like a fool. Besides, I made you a sandwich. Was it my fault you dropped it overboard?"

"Soaked bread's so hard to hold," Clyde shrugged. "Ever try to gaff a piece of cheese, Vady? I'm so hungry now I could eat a sea cucumber."

We followed them out on deck. The lights of a boat were just coming into the harbor. We walked around the scow as Carl Henning came up to the fishhouse.

As the lights from the scow shone down on his deck, we stood there gaping, unable to believe what we saw. In all our summer's fishing we'd never seen a load like this! Huge kings filled his checkers and overflowed onto the deck! They were piled in tiers from cockpit to pilot-house.

"Holy gee!" Clyde exploded. "Where did you get those?"

"Not so loud," Carl warned. "We don't want the others to hear. They'll catch on soon enough. The kings are in at Coronation. You fellows be ready to follow me out about three in the morning."

We dashed back to the boat to get what sleep we could before it was time to leave.

Getting up at three in the morning is no cinch at any time. Now that the days were shorter, it would be a long time until dawn. We groped around in the chill of the galley to find the kerosene lantern that cast its dim beams for us to dress by.

Even in this shivery hour Vady was talkative and cheer-ful, until he remembered that in the excitement of the previous evening he'd forgotten to gas up.

"I wouldn't wake Lefty at this time of night," he said. "Perhaps we can run over later in the day." He looked like a disappointed kid as he stood in the pilothouse watching the lights of the other boats disappearing in the gloom.

Secretly I was glad for one more day's reprieve. Many were the tales we had heard of the Coronation Flats, none of them reassuring. Sudden storms and heavy tide rips had taken their toll. Boats had capsized and fishermen drowned. Good harbors were lacking, although it was said that old-timers could find some protection among the uncharted bights and coves of the Spanish Islands. We weren't old-timers, and I thought we might never be if we fished the treacherous waters of the Coronation Flats.

It was ten o'clock by the time we were gassed up and ready to leave. Even though the fog hung low over the water, blotting everything from sight, Vady was all for starting for Coronation.

I talked hard and fast.

"You know how fish are," I said, "here today and gone tomorrow. It would be too foggy to fish even if we could find our way out there. What if Carl did hit a school? He's not likely to find them again today."

"Carl didn't hit a school," Vady denied, "the kings are there, the fall run we've been waiting for. Now you don't want to go because there's a little fog." His voice was sharp.

"I'm satisfied," I snapped back. "We've been making good, averaging over forty dollars a day. How come you're so money-mad?"

"It's not the money. I'd like to get into some good fishing for once. All summer it's been the same—either you want to run in early when the fish are hitting, or you're scared, or you insist on running off on a wild-goose chase."

"I wish I'd stayed home!" I choked, realizing how unutterably weary I was of the long hours, the discomfort of the boat, the everlasting chill and dampness, and my nagging fear of the water. At that moment I could gladly have given up all hope of Eternal Glory for one glimpse of the wanigan.

"I wish you had!" Vady said, to my shocked surprise. "I should have known better than to bring you in the first place. You never have had the right idea about this game. A fellow doesn't fish just to catch a few fish. He fishes to catch all the fish it's possible to get. You knew the hours would be long. They have to be, in a short season."

When the fog lifted we went out and fished around Hardscrabble until dusk. We passed the day in dignified silence.

As we went in, the evening effects were beautiful. The wind had died down, leaving glassy swells. The mountains gradually changed from green to hazy blue, then mauve, with shadows in every shade from lavender to deep purple. The colors of the sunset were past telling, their reflections making a quivering rainbow into the harbor. Even the gulls, drifting lazily over the boat, were lavender in the glow. Surely this was a vision from some forgotten world. Bathed in the beauty of the scene, our misunderstandings of the morning seemed a trifling thing.

"Honey," I said, sitting down on the hatch cover, "I'm sorry about this morning, but the fog terrifies me. There isn't much time left. We'll go to Coronation in the morning and stay as long as you like."

"I've been sorry too," Vady said with his ready smile. "It's hard to explain how I feel about fishing. It's not the money. I don't care about that. It's the thrill and excitement of catching them, the challenge of trying to get just one more. It must be the same urge that makes some men stalk lions, or that the Indians had when they chased buffalo across the plains. The instinct for food, I suppose.

My whole nature seems to change. It's like a fever. All I can think of is fish and more fish. I can't expect you to understand, Betsy, because I don't understand it myself. All I know is, it isn't important. We've done well enough, and what if we hadn't? Having each other is all that matters, yet I keep you out here when I know you want to go in."

"I haven't been a good partner . . ." I began.

"Yes, you have. Fishing without you wouldn't be any fun at all. I know you're nervous and worn out. I know you're afraid of the water. If you say so, we'll forget Coronation, start for home right now."

"I don't say so. Of course we'll go to Coronation."

It was well after dark when Carl and the *Skookum* got in. Clyde was jubilant. And why not? More than a thousand pounds of future Friday dinners! Three hundred forty dollars and seventy cents in good American coin!

"What a day!" he gloated. "Why didn't you come out? The darned things were everywhere! This afternoon I hooked into the biggest soaker I ever saw! I knew I'd never get it in alive, so I called Nina to bring the gun. No answer. I was yarding him in inch by inch, hoping he'd wear himself out. Then I'd let him run when he got too wild. I kept working him toward the boat, hoping to get the gaff at him, yelling to Nina whenever I could get a breath. My tongue hung out so far I could have stropped my razor on it. My arms felt like two toothaches. I reached for the gaff and he saw me. He took off with a spurt, like a porpoise, made a pass around the other line and headed back. When the slack took up in the leader it stopped him. I hurled the gaff at the cabin to wake Nina up. The fish must have jumped five feet in the air! He looked me in the eye. With a sneer he was gone, hook, line, sinker and spoon! I cooled off, then went below to view the corpse, thinking of course the little lady was dead. Guess what I saw?"

"Couldn't possibly," Vady laughed.

"There was my little frau, all cozy on the bunk, stirring a batch of fudge for her pampered husband."

"Wives are wonderful institutions," Vady said. There was a twinkle in his eye that made me wonder exactly what he meant.

Chapter 22

We left next morning while it was still dark. At six we dropped our lines off Helm Point, the southern extremity of Coronation Island. This bold headland, so different in appearance from the other points and capes we'd become accustomed to, can be seen for many miles at sea. It is a well-known landmark for boats plying the outside waterways. Rising sheer in high, weather-beaten cliffs, it flattens off into tablelands. No vegetation shows on the bare rocks, which are highly colored in yellows, reds, and browns. Numerous caves and caverns form dark patches of indigo along its face. Thousands of sea birds nest among the rocks, darting along the cliffs and filling the sky as they circle over the water. Breakers offshore leap from the foam at their base, ugly sea monsters fighting the ocean swells.

This was the sight we saw in the gray dawn. Down dropped my spirits like a shaft of mercury in a sudden freeze, with the realization that here was our fishing grounds—here on the edge of the unpacific Pacific.

Oh yes, we'd had our breakfast! After our talk of the previous day I'd jumped out of the bunk willingly enough. Hadn't Vady promised there'd be no more stalling around at quitting time? By getting in early tonight we could make up for the sleep we'd lost.

Vady whistled in the cockpit, making up spare gear.

"Are you getting ready for next summer?" I asked him. "What do you expect to do with all those leaders, now that the season is nearly over?"

"This won't be many when we get into the fish. Those big ones kink the leaders, break the nylon, straighten out hooks, run around the lines, and mess things up generally. Get me a box of Number Eights. I'm going to put on new hooks all around."

"Some fish! Perhaps we won't even get a bite. Could happen, you know. Carl and Clyde aren't getting them," I pointed out as the *Skookum* passed us and Clyde shook his head.

Just then we heard Clyde shout. "Got him!" he yelled, going into action.

"We're in 'em!" Vady leaped for the gurdy as a pole arced slowly down. "Bottom!" he said in disgust as the line snapped loose. "We're in too close. Get out of here, quick."

Carl had warned us. "She's humpy as a camel caravan," he'd said. "Pick out your landmarks onshore or stay well out from the point."

We headed out. The *Emblem* rolled in the swell. Far

out over the sea the horizon was obscured by a blanket of fog, murky and yellow. There was a filmy sheen on the water like thick oil on the surface of a pool. A few wispy clouds drifted in a sky that was neither blue nor gray. A day no better or worse than many we had fished, yet it was stifling and oppressive, as if the very world were holding its breath.

A pole went down with a jerk that made the boat tremble. There was a whoop from the cockpit! "Yippee! We're in 'em at last! Give me a hand, Babe. Coil those leaders and get 'em out of the way." He reached for the snap-on, gaffed the fish, and threw it on deck. It slapped against my leg and slithered across the boards.

"Sixty pounders!" I sniffed. "Looks like about a ten-pound coho to me."

"Don't just stand there," Vady said, busy with another line. "Take the hook out. Put the fish in the checker. Find me that long-handled gaff. Bring some spoons—Superiors, the big ones."

The gurdy ground on and on while Vady, his lean face tense with excitement, worked at top speed. So this was it! The reason small boys sit beside some quiet stream, dabbling for hours with a piece of string and a bent pin; the urge that drives those same boys, grown to manhood, into untold hardships with battling waves and freezing gear. The irresistible attraction of fishing, whether for minnows or for whales. Yes, this was it, and they could have it, I thought, as I leaned to pick a fish from the deck and got a slimy slap across the face.

"Don't just stand there," Vady said again. "Slide those fish into the far checker. I'll need more room. Slosh down the deck before you break your neck. Move that knife out of my way. Find me a ten-pound lead."

Blood and slime splattered his face and clothes. Sweat trickled from beneath his hat.

"Look at that main pole! Good Lord! We've snagged a whale! Look at that baby take it!"

"Do something. It's bottom. No fish could bend a pole like that." I started for the pilothouse.

"Bottom, hell! It's a fish. I can feel it!"

"Then reel it in. What's the matter with you? Paralyzed?"

"Let me handle this," Vady said with dignity. "Let him fight that lead for a while. It may take some of the ginger out of him."

The line slackened. Instantly Vady threw in the clutch. The line came in easily. No jerk, no tug.

"Gone!" Vady groaned. "I knew it. I've never been able to hold one of those big babies."

Then, not ten feet behind the boat, the water exploded in a crystal shower. There was a flash of green and blue as the fish leaped into the air. But it led up like a lamb on a ribbon and nestled beside the boat just below the surface.

"Good God!" Vady breathed.

I looked over the side and could hardly believe what I saw. Magnified by the water, that fish looked as big as a shark! Its blue-green back lightened to silver along its belly. The hump of its jaw almost hid the spoon, well snagged in its lower jaw. Its eyes, yellow and opalescent, seemed to stare straight into mine.

Vady reached for the gaff and cautiously grasped the leader. At that the water broke into foam. Spray showered the deck.

The line ran out as the fish sounded. It quivered like a tight fiddle string with the strain. Twenty fathoms of steel line and forty pounds of lead were nothing but playthings for that king.

Ever so slowly the gurdy began to reel in. Grind, grind, grind, as the fish fought against it. "He's tiring," Vady said.

But not that fish! Twenty feet from the boat he took off again in a series of wild leaps and runs.

"I'll have to let him take it," Vady said. "I've got to play him out if I ever land him."

"The lines are full," I told him, pointing to the poles. "Why don't you leave him and pull the others?"

He gave me a scornful glance. "Take a chance on losing that fellow? You're crazy."

Four times Vady had him close to the boat, only to have him take off and head for the bottom again. There was determination on his face as he put the clutch in for the fifth round. This was evidently the salmon's last chance for freedom. Plainly he was tiring. His runs were shorter and less frequent.

As the king came up beside the boat, Vady reached for the gaff. Slowly he tightened up on the leader. At last he had the head out of water. He swung with all his might. The king quivered and lay still.

Together we dragged it into the checker. The biggest salmon I'd ever seen! His nose touched one end of the checker, and his tail extended a good six inches beyond the other end. Here was a good day's wages, enough fish to feed fifty hungry men!

"How much will he weigh?"

But Vady had no time for questions now. He was already busy on the other lines. I'd have to wait for that king's weight until he filled the scales on the scow.

I glanced at my watch. One o'clock! Where had the

day gone? The fish had slacked off. Vady picked up the knife and ran a file along its edge.

"Did you ever see anything like this?" he laughed shakily, his hands trembling. We were both tired. The checkers were full of fish. If we started back now we could troll in and still reach Fisherman's Harbor before dark.

The sky had become overcast; great, dark masses of clouds rolled up in the south. A yellow haze cast a strange light over the water. Far above us gulls circled and wheeled, and in the distance a school of porpoises came toward us, cutting the water in knife-clean spurts.

"The fish seem to have quit," I said, making it sound casual.

"They always slack off in the middle of the day. This will give me a chance to clean. Let's see if this is a red," and he reached for our prize.

He slit the belly and the flesh fell back, deep coral and firm! The perfect fish, inside and out.

"We'll go farther out this afternoon. Maybe we can hook the mate to this one."

His resolution of yesterday was forgotten. Surely we had enough for one day. All those fish worth from six to fifteen dollars each. And the big one! Eighteen—twenty?

"We're 'way over a hundred dollars. We've passed our goal."

"Easily," Vady agreed. "We'll double it before night." He threw his tattered gloves over the side and reached for another pair.

"It gets dark by seven now," I hinted, "and it's after one now. Besides, the weather looks threatening."

"It looks all right to me. These ocean swells don't mean anything." The knife flashed as he removed a gill with a deft twist. "What of it? It's worth it, isn't it?"

"The gulls are soaring," I said desperately, "and look, porpoises playing around the boat."

"Are they? I didn't notice."

"It's such a long run back, how would it be if we trolled—"

"For God's sake!" Vady exploded. 'So that's what you're getting at. You want to quit! Quit, and run in. The first good fishing we've had. Our chance to make the summer pay."

Wearily I went into the pilothouse. He was right. I'd been the one who wanted to make it pay. The one who'd said it couldn't be done. Of course I tried to justify myself in my own mind. He shouldn't get so tired. We really didn't need the money so badly.

I jumped nervously as a porpoise cut the water beside us. The fog was closer now. If we went out there it would cover us like a load of wet feathers, smothering out the world. The farther boats were already lost to sight.

What would he do if I took things into my own hands and turned the boat toward harbor anyway? We'd argue, of course. Say things we didn't mean. Later it would all seem like a joke as we talked it over and decided it didn't matter. But would it? Would we laugh? Perhaps not. Perhaps one couldn't destroy a dream without creating a corpse. After all, my fears might be ungrounded. There was no wind, and the swells were as glassily smooth as before—although perceptibly larger than in the morning. The *Emblem* was larger than Carl's boat or the *Skookum,* and they weren't heading in. Must I always be a coward?

Reluctantly I turned the wheel. We headed out to sea. Almost at once we were in the fish again!

All afternoon they slapped on deck. The checkers filled and I emptied them, piling the fish on deck. Vady kept up the mad pace, no time to hail the passing boats this day, no time to clean those piles of fish.

His gloves were in shreds again, but he wouldn't stop to change them. No butcher every looked more gory. His face, weary and drawn, was coated with blood and flecks of salt. And this was fun! Something to fight for and enjoy!

At four o'clock the *Skookum* passed us, heading home. Her poles were up, her decks loaded. As she lurched into a trough of the sea, I noticed with dismay that only her poles and pilothouse showed above the top of the wave.

At four-thirty Carl and two other boats went by, harbor-bound. As Carl stepped out on deck to wave in passing, a sudden gust of wind blew his hat far out over the water.

At five I strained my eyes through the mist. No boats were in sight. We were alone in Iphigenia Bay!

As the wind picked up it became more and more difficult to detect a strike. The poles jerked constantly with the rolling of the boat. Vady could hardly keep his footing in the slippery cockpit. He slipped and went down on his knee. He got up like an old man.

"I guess we've had enough," he said, coming to the pilothouse door. "My arms and hands are so stiff I can hardly handle the lines, and I still have all that cleaning to do. I'll pick up. You can head in."

Through the fog I could barely make out the bulky outline of Helm Point, first leg on the long trip in. The swells were choppy now, not smooth and oily as before. As Vady put up the poles he took an extra wrap around the mast, securing them tightly.

"It'll be dark when we get in," I told him. "All the boats have left."

"Why didn't you mention it? It looks like it's making up for a blow. We should have gone with them."

I should have told him? I wouldn't have dared!

"I'll take the wheel," he said. "How about some coffee?"

We hadn't eaten since breakfast, but when I went down to the galley I found it much too rough to think of making a fire in the stove.

"I'll go out and put the fish down in the hold," Vady said, "secure the skiff and tighten everything down."

The *Emblem* bucked into the storm. Awake now after her lazy day, she charged forward to meet the waves. Plunging her nose into green water, she rose to shake the foam from her bow.

The noise was terrific—the roar of the wind, the creak and groan of the straining boat, the slosh of water across the deck, and the intermittent banging of the deck bucket as it slid back and forth against the coaming.

It seemed to me Vady had been gone on deck for ages. What could be taking him so long? I didn't dare leave the wheel, even for a quick look outside.

A wall of green water towered over us, hung for an agonized moment, and toppled. The *Emblem* shuddered. The pilothouse trembled as the water swept against it. I watched the little streams that trickled from the coils of the shore line lying on the forward deck, and the thought came to me that it was strange to see frayed ends on a line. Vady usually put in a wall knot or whipped them. The next wave would probably wash it over anyway, so it didn't matter now. I wouldn't tell him, and risk the chance he'd take by going up on the bow to fasten it or bring it in. We could always get another shore line.

The strait was smoking. The gale picked the tops off the whitecaps, and the spindrift scudded across the water in a misty spray. But ahead the water was black and forbidding with watery giants leaping in all directions, rearing their heads to mighty heights, only to fall back of their own weight. The rip tides of Sumner Strait!

Could we hold the boat on course when we hit that water?

Should we turn back? But if we did, where could we go? These harbors, hidden among the islands, would give us scant protection even if we found them.

Then Vady pushed in beside me, smelling strong of fish, and took the wheel. He slowed the boat and headed into the rips.

Crouching on the galley steps, soaked to the skin by the dashing spray, I thought, There is nothing now between us and eternity but the strength of the *Emblem.* This boat, so sturdy in a quiet harbor, so frail in this boiling sea.

"We've lost the shore line! When did that go over?" He seemed unnecessarily agitated about it. What did an extra shore line matter in this caldron?

Too scared to speak, I shook my head.

"Brace up," he said. "We're all right. Hold on a little longer and we'll soon be out of it."

How long was soon? Were we making any headway? We seemed to be standing still, pounding and rolling and gaining nothing. The steady throb of the motor missed a beat. It slowed, picked up, slowed again. And then it stopped!

Vady tried the starter but there was no answering whir. He went below.

So this was the end! The *Emblem* had turned sidewise. She rolled sickeningly. How long would we drift at the mercy of these hissing waves, with the boat lifting sluggishly after every battering blow?

He squeezed out beside me and with the flashlight in his hand made his way to the cockpit.

I heard him call.

Sobbing with fright, I crawled along the deck, grasping the coaming with both hands. He grabbed my hand and helped me into the cockpit.

"Something's fouled the propeller," he shouted. "I think that line. Hold the flashlight if you can. We have to get it off."

The flashlight wasn't much use. Its faint beam showed thinly on the dark water.

Leaning far over the stern, Vady groped with the pike pole, trying to find a loose end of the rope. Back and forth through the water. To the right, to the left, pushing it down as far as he could reach.

"I've got it! I've got it!" he shouted. "Easy now. Watch out! If we can get it in–"

Slowly he raised the pole. The line lay across it in a loose loop. He pulled it slowly toward the boat. Black fingers of water reached greedily toward it. Getting that line was our only hope of survival.

He reached out, grabbed it, handed it to me.

"Pull it in. Be careful. For God's sake don't let go. I'll turn the shaft by hand. We'll work it off."

While Vady turned the shaft below I pulled at the rope, hoping and praying that with each tug it would come loose. At last it did! Over the side came the wet, frazzled end. Lucky for us Vady had left the dangling ends and clumsy knot that had prevented it from winding farther on the shaft.

As suddenly as it had come up the wind died down. When the motor started, as it did with the first try after we had worked off the rope, we were already nearly out of the rip.

Lights blazed on the scow as we came into the harbor. A packer lay at the dock, loading fish for the trip to Ketchikan.

Still dazed from our frightening experience, I heard Lefty's shout of welcome. "I thought you'd holed in," he said. "I didn't expect to see you back tonight. Quite a blow."

"We had a little trouble," Vady said.

A little trouble! Then all it had meant to him was delay and annoyance. That hideous nightmare! A little trouble!

"The wind's about died down. Looks like it would be all right tomorrow. I've got all these fish to clean. Won't get much sleep tonight."

I knew then I had reached the end of my endurance. Neither my mind nor my body could be forced into facing another day like the one we had just gone through.

When the packer left, she would have a passenger for Ketchikan.

Chapter 23

I went shakily down the ladder into the galley. All the strength seemed to have gone out of my legs. I got out a sea bag and began stuffing things into it, not knowing or caring what things. Clothes, toothbrush, shoes, pajamas, I jammed them in and closed the bag with a yank on the string.

I looked up as I heard Vady come in from the deck. "What's going on? What are you doing?" he asked. His voice was hollow, his sunken eyes dull. For a minute I was tempted to give up my plan. But only for a minute.

"I can't stand it!" I cried, my voice rising to a shriek. "The wind—the boat—the fish—"

"Take it easy, Babe," Vady said as I burst into tears.

"That won't help. These things happen. Tomorrow's another day."

Tomorrow! Yes, tomorrow was another day. Another day of dismal fog, of gray waves slapping against the side of the boat, of weariness and fear, of fish, and the long run back to the scow in the dark.

"Come on," Vady said, "you're tired. Lie down on the bunk."

How funny he'd tell me to lie down when I was going home. I started to laugh and couldn't stop.

Vady put his arms around me and held me tight. He gave me a little shake. "Snap out of it," he said.

"I want to go h-o-m-e," I wailed, laughing and crying at the same time.

"Then go," Vady said. "I've got to clean those fish." He picked up the sea bag and carried it out on deck.

The skipper of the packer was obliging. He graciously gave up his cabin to me, going below to bunk with the crew. As the boat left the harbor I crawled into the bunk. It wasn't the best bed in the world, with its greasy blankets and slipless pillow, but to me it was like sleeping on a cloud.

There were two other passengers, I found out next morning when I went down to the galley—two long-haired fishermen who had left their boat farther north and were hitch-cruising to Seattle, and who, after a season of fishing together, were noticeably cool to each other.

The crew were the engineer, smudged with grease and oil, a "dese and dose, dis and dat" Brooklynese; the skipper, red-eyed and morose, lean and weather-beaten of skin, with a thin mouth shaped by profanity; and Cookie, who had been a deck hand the night before, helping with the fish-loading. He was a dark-skinned breed with a sparse black beard and flashing black eyes.

Now he swayed over the sink, keeping his equilibrium by sheer will power.

"A pirate's den if I ever saw one," I thought as I sized up my traveling companions. I took a place at the table and helped myself to the really excellent hot cakes. No one looked up or spoke.

Then came the explosion!

The skipper jumped to his feet. He gave Cookie a shove that sent him spinning against the sink. "Get on with those dishes, you damned so-and-so!" he barked. "Every time we get in port you get drunk as a coot and let your work go. Get at 'em, I say, so you can stand your watch. I'm getting damned tired of this!"

"Shut your trap," Cookie warbled back, "before I wrap the soup around your neck."

The skipper slammed out the door with a backward glare.

Cookie squelched a burp behind a grimy hand. "He doesn't mean a thing," he chortled fondly. "Him and me's just like that," holding up two crossed fingers. "We been workin' together for years."

In Alaska the ties of friendship are strong. Yes, and robust.

Cookie was garrulous. While I wiped dishes with a rag that might have come out of the engine room and was used for everything from floor to stove, he tried his best to make me feel at home.

"I gotta have my teeth pulled when we get to Ketchikan," he confided. "Ain't nothin' left but a bunch of snags. See?" and he dragged his lower lip down to expose his snaggled, yellowed teeth. "False teeth are a bother, though. Expensive, too. Had a friend got hisself a pair. Cost him a hundred 'n' sixty dollars. Scuse me, lady!" as a burp caught up with him. Cookie was genteel.

He wiped his mouth on a dish towel, slipped it under his belt, and went on with his story. "Old Cockeye, that's my friend, Cockeye Wilson, he got drunk. He's so fat he uses a winch to get into his pants. Well, he got to laughin' and he doubled up. His teeth fell outa his pocket and they hit the water. They drowneded, and Cockeye had to go buy hisself another pair. You're bound to lose 'em, and every time it costs you money. Put 'em in your shirt pocket, they fall out when you lean. Put 'em in your pants pocket, they bite you when you set. They just ain't no way to keep 'em safe," he ended sadly.

All but one of the long-hairs had left the galley. Now he got up from the table muttering, "I believe you, but there's thousands and thousands who wouldn't," he slammed out on deck.

"Riled," Cookie explained. "Poor summer. Couple'a boys, fifteen, sixteen, outfished the whole shebang at Alexander. Had an old pot woulda' scart a duck to ride in. Even outfished Swivel-neck George, best fisherman in Alaska."

He burped again and reached for his bottle. "Want a drink, lady?" extending the bottle politely. "I'm sure dry."

"Thank you, no," I told him. "I think I'll go on deck."

Anxious to get home, I begrudged the time we lost when we stopped to pick up a fish scow to tow into Craig. Then, when we had already lost several hours, we had to wait while the skipper made the rounds of the town, looking up old friends and acquaintances. It was four o'clock in the evening before we got under way again. Cookie, whom I'd come to know very well, as the galley was the only warm place on the packer, assured me that we would reach Ketchikan by morning, six o'clock at the latest.

One hour out from Craig I heard a sound so familiar

I thought for a moment I was back on the *Emblem.* Br-r-r! Chug, rattle! Silence. We were drifting. Could it be that Diesels were allergic to me?

The engineer, who was at the wheel, ran below. The skipper, his thin mouth pouring out a stream of short, terse words, followed. Cookie stuck his head out the galley door and bellowed, "What the hell's up now?" The long-hairs looked resigned. Knowing the routine so well, I merely waited.

But here was a definite improvement over the *Emblem.* Instead of a sheet on the mast, two toots of her whistle brought a passing tender quickly to our side. How natural it seemed to go back to Craig on the end of a towline!

If I hurried uptown, I might be able to catch the last plane of the day to Ketchikan! But it took forever to get alongside the dock, then the tide was out and I had to scramble up the long ladder to the wharf. The last plane had left, ten minutes before.

All evening I walked through town, asking those I met whether they knew of a room I might get for the night. While everyone was sympathetic, there were just no rooms to be had.

There was no place where I could sit all night. Not even a park with a bench to curl up on. In desperation I went back to the boat. Cookie, alone in the galley, welcomed me as heartily as if I'd been a bootlegger with a bulging hip pocket. When the skipper came in, he insisted I take his room again, refusing any pay for the trip or the food. Pirates? Maybe in looks, but kindhearted pirates withal. True Alaskans at heart.

In the morning we learned it would take at least a day to get the packer running again. Planes were all grounded by fog. Would I ever get home? At three in the afternoon it began to clear and a plane came in. By five I was home, in the wanigan. My first season's fishing was over!

I worried about Vady, of course, picturing those awful seas. They haunted my dreams. I woke at night with the memory of green water breaking over the bow of the boat. Where was he now? Out there alone, steering the boat, catching the fish, making the long run at night and in the morning, cooking his own meals, throwing himself down on the bunk for a few hours' sleep.

Had he been a little cool when I left, or had I only imagined it in my overwrought state? Who could blame him if he had been, when I'd run out on him as I had—and those foolish hysterics on top of it all. How would he greet me when he came home? Would he be indifferent and unwilling to talk? Or would he tell me what a poor sport I'd been? Why wasn't I more like Nina, calm and unruffled no matter how rough the water? What if she did forget to feed Clyde sometimes? She was able to pull fish while he made his own sandwiches.

What would the future bring? Would we fish together next season or would Vady refuse to have me with him? And if he did want me to go, would I want to? Surprisingly enough, the answer was yes. With fear in my heart and a knot in my stomach, I'd go to see, again, the splendor of a sunset, the moonlight on a quiet bay, the wild, tumbling waters of a mountain stream, the sweep of the ocean or the magic beauty of some hidden inlet. I'd go for the humor and fellowship aboard the boats and at the scow, and with admiration for the fishermen.

I'd go for the biggest reward of all, my husband's companionship at day's end when, after a hearty meal, he and I would sit in the crowded little galley talking over the day's adventures. There'd be new dangers, new disappointments, other arguments and misunderstandings, but I'd go.

But such thoughts didn't fill all my time. Being at home was a delight. How could anyone complain of the monotony of housework? Just to be able to move around freely was pleasure enough, but to sleep in a bed that stood solid all night! Bliss! Tide, weather, wind—at last they had no importance.

One day in town I met Mr. Dobbs. He had just come in. Vady, he told me, was on his way in with the Lindens, coming from the north. Dobbs had come by way of Cape Chacon. He had startling news. He had picked Johnny up at Kaigani on the way in so the two boats could run together. As they rounded the cape in a calm sea, he looked over to the other boat and saw she was low in the water. Turning, he ran close alongside just as the water washed over her bow. Johnny jumped to the deck of the *Dobbs.* Chicken coop awash, stern high, and motor running, old *Stinky* went under to disappear forever in Davy Jones's locker.

I watched the narrows closely, going to the window a hundred times a day. It was two weeks after I had left when Vady came home. The boats reached Ketchikan at night, so I didn't see them pass, and didn't know he was home until he came through the door.

He was smiling! He grabbed me in his arms, his manner the same as if he'd just been to town for the day.

We lingered long over his supper. His catch for the two weeks had totaled nearly fourteen hundred dollars! "The best king run in years," he told me. "I caught a lot of big ones after you left, but nothing like the prize. He weighed over sixty-one pounds."

We got out the budget book, tattered and torn from its summer on the boat.

"As near as I can tell," he said, "we've cleared about two thousand dollars for the season. Not bad."

"I didn't think we'd make expenses, with all our troubles."

"I told you we could do it," my husband said. "When will you learn to believe Daddy? I've been thinking," he went on, "ever since you left. Marriage is a business of give-and-take. It has to be that way. I know you didn't enjoy fishing. It's a hard, dangerous game. Now it's your turn. We don't need to fish for a living. There are plenty of other things we can do."

"You mean you'd go back to the States?"

"Sure. I can't say I want to, but if it would make you happier . . ."

"Oh yes! I do like Alaska, but I'd rather be in the States."

"I've had my summer of fishing. Now we'll have what you want."

"A little house! It wouldn't have to be much, just something comfortable and cozy, with room for a garden and flowers. A place to keep for the rest of our lives."

"It doesn't sound like too much to ask for," Vady said with a grin.

The days passed quickly as I looked ahead. We'd soon be back home, back to familiar scenes, warmth and sunshine, old friends, where we could visit with Bev and Harvey and see our grandchildren whenever we wanted to. With a "For Sale" sign on the *Emblem* I felt it wouldn't be long.

Vady came home one day at noon. "You've been up to something," I said when I saw his face. "Come on, out with it. You couldn't be mysterious if you tried."

"We sold the *Emblem,*" he said.

He'd sold the *Emblem!* Although it was what I'd been

hoping for, a strange feeling of sadness went over me. She'd been part of our lives and, cranky and stubborn as she was, we'd loved her.

"Got six thousand for her," Vady said.

"Twice as much as we paid for her! That's a good down payment on a house and enough to keep the wolf from the door until we get settled. That, and what we get from the wanigan."

"Wait," Vady said, "I haven't told you quite all. I bought something too. I bought a scow."

"A scow! What kind of scow?"

"A fish-buying scow. It was such a marvelous opportunity I didn't dare pass it up. You know how badly it's needed at Kaigani. Think of the chances, Babe! We'll live right on it, probably stay out there winter and summer."

A picture was slowly forming in my mind. A fish scow, far back on the end of a towline, was moving slowly down Clarence Strait. Now it was off Chacon, wallowing in the tide rips. It was passing the Nunez breakers with twenty-five long miles ahead to its destination. It was lying in Kaigani Harbor, rolling gently in the swell of a southeaster. In a tiny kitchen I was preparing a meal. The scow rolled, a kettle crashed to the floor. . . .

"What's the matter, Babe?" my husband laughed. "Don't you like the idea?"

How could I have thought anything could change him? Had anything changed me? No, we were still two parallel lines, traveling along side by side but never meeting. Fortunate indeed for our marriage that at least we were congenial lines.

"You'll like it," he assured me. "There won't be much for you to do. We'll have a store aboard and you can take care of that, pay off the fishermen, keep the books. Housekeeping doesn't amount to a darn in a place like that. Oh, if we have a big run sometimes you might have to help ice the fish at night. But most of the time you can just set your easel on the deck and paint all day!"

How many times had I seen that look on my husband's face? That boundless enthusiasm for the thing that was coming next.

Scows, fishing boats, homes, what difference did it make, after all? Apart we were nothing. Together we could still lick the world.